HEART

HUNGER

CINDI McMENAMIN

Cindi McMenamin (signature)

HARVEST HOUSE PUBLISHERS
Eugene, Oregon 97402

Cover by Koechel Peterson & Associates, Minneapolis, Minnesota

Photograph courtesy of Photonica/Kamil Vojnar

Heart Hunger
Copyright © 2000 by Cindi McMenamin
Published by Harvest House Publishers
Eugene, Oregon 97402

Library of Congress Cataloging-in-Publications Data
McMenamin, Cindi, 1965-
      Heart Hunger / Cindi McMenamin.
         p.   cm.
      Includes bibliographical references.
      ISBN 0-7369-0184-1
      1. Christian Women—Religious life. I. Title.
BV4527.M43 2000   99-41565
248.8'43—dc21   CIP

Printed in the United States of America.

00 01 02 03 04 /BC/ 10 9 8 7 6 5 4 3 2 1

For my daughter, Dana Katherine,
and
for women, everywhere,
who long for something more...

Acknowledgments

My heartfelt thanks to...

- the special women who have let me share their stories throughout the pages of this book so that others might come to a better understanding of our Savior's love.

- my parents for letting me share the "untold stories" of our past for the sake of God's glory.

- my husband, Hugh, for loving me, encouraging me, and believing in my dream.

- my editor, Steve Miller, whose good eye, gentle encouragement, and gracious enthusiasm guided me through this project.

And I am forever grateful to the Lord Jesus Christ for giving me the inspiration and the words...and for being the Lover of my Soul.

Contents

Longing for Love

Dream with me, for a moment, about the perfect man:

He's my protector. My provider. He gives me security and soothes my nerves after a rough day. He rejuvenates me and encourages me, just when I need it. And he points me in the right direction with wonderful, godly advice. Although I fear the future or my own failure at times, I don't need to. He's always by my side, both physically and emotionally to get me through what lies ahead. He comforts me and puts me at ease when I face tension or opposition. He makes me feel special and called, assuring me of my purpose in life. His love for me is all I will ever need. I'm confident that I will experience happiness and joy the rest of my life because he and I will be together forever.

Sounds too good to be true, doesn't it? But, finding that kind of fulfillment in love is possible for me *and* for you. That's because the "Dream Man" I described really exists. My description is actually a paraphrase of Psalm 23 in today's language—a psalm written thousands of years ago by a young shepherd boy named David about the God he had come to know intimately. You and I, as women longing for more, can know the Lord Jesus as our "Perfect Husband," just as David knew Him as his "Good Shepherd."

Unfortunately, it took several years for me to come to the realization that the Lord—not my husband, friend, or anyone else—must be the One to meet my needs. For years, I refused to give in to the idea that my Prince Charming was lacking in some way. After all, I had married a man who communicated beautifully through letters, demonstrated tenderness just when I needed it, and responded to my needs in a sensitive and loving way. For four years, we were in wedded bliss! Then two things happened: He became a full-time pastor and I became a full-time mother. He suddenly faced the pressure of meeting the spiritual needs of a new congregation and was soon preoccupied and, at times, overwhelmed. I was at home with an infant, adjusting to the changes in my life, feeling neglected by my husband and longing for some emotional connection.

The problem was that I wasn't going to the Lord for my fulfillment. I was looking to a person—my husband—to fill the emotional void in my life. For that matter, any time we look to a person for our fulfillment—a friend, lover, parent, child, or anyone else—we end up feeling shortchanged because, as we will see throughout the pages of this book, no one but the Lord can satisfy.

Refusing to admit my husband was *unable* to meet my needs, I continued to press him to try harder. He began feeling more and more like he couldn't make the mark with me. And I began to feel that our situation was hopeless. Through frustration, disappointment, and much prayer and study of the Word I finally came face-to-face with the realization that my husband—and anyone else, for that matter—will never be able to be all I expect and need of him. He can't pick up on my insecurities and fill the void that wells up inside me sometimes. He can't read my mind and know what I need to hear to make me feel loved and comforted. He can't be my all-in-all so I can go on facing life as a confident, capable woman. And he wasn't meant to do all that. My husband was meant to be my partner, not my Emotional Provider. He was meant to be my friend, not my Source of Fulfillment. God let him be my lover, not my Sustainer. Those other roles can only be filled by the Lord.

When I finally realized that my Prince Charming was not the God-man I had believed him to be, I wasn't bitter or disappointed. I was, instead, relieved to find that I no longer had to be disappointed with unrealistic expectations. I no longer had to struggle with emotional longings that had long gone unfulfilled. My husband was relieved, too. When I placed my expectations with the Lord, where they should be, I became a little more lovable in his sight.

I have seen the Lord come through time and again for the lonely in love. Not only with me, but in the lives and hearts of countless women. For the past ten years, women have come to me with empty hearts, longing to find in their relationships the intimacy that will make them feel whole. None of those women ever found it...until they became intimate with the Lord.

You can find this kind of intimacy that leads to fulfillment, too, by establishing a deeply personal relationship with the Lord. But with any relationship, you must get off to the right start with your new love, grow together, and then go the distance. This book will guide you through three phases to help you establish and maintain a healthy relationship with God:

Getting Started—In the first four chapters, you will see how you can get started by responding to God's invitation to become intimate with Him. You will begin to see Him as the Only One who satisfies, and you will learn about how He accepts you unconditionally and how you can find security in your relationship with Him and how He sees you as beautiful and new.

Growing Together—In chapters five through nine, you will get to know Him better by discovering how to pour out your heart to Him, how to be His best friend, how to please Him and how to listen to His loving voice.

Going the Distance—In the remaining three chapters, you will discover the type of future you have with the Lord by looking at what He offers you, what He expects of you in your relationship with Him, and where the two of you are headed in a lifetime of commitment together.

Whether you're single and still looking, happily or unhappily married, divorced and hurting, or widowed with no regrets, you have longings—longings for love, companionship, and intimacy. The Lord Jesus Christ stands ready to meet those longings and fulfill your greatest hunger. But only until you see Him as your ultimate Source of Satisfaction, grow with Him and go the distance with Him, will you finally be filled. Filled and satisfied and longing no more.

Come with me, my friend, as we explore the depths of God's heart and together find True Love.

Part I

Getting Started

Are you ready to meet the Only One who can
satisfy? Let me introduce you to the Lover of your
soul, who waits for you with open arms. You will
find that He loves you unconditionally, He accepts
you for who you really are, and He will never
leave you. You will see yourself as He sees you
and realize there is nothing you can do to lose
His love. You're heading for a wonderful
adventure in finding True Love.
And it all starts here.

1
Finding the One Who Will Satisfy

Judy never thought she could feel so alone. Somewhere along the road, in the three years she had been married, her husband Mark had stopped talking. The freshness between them had grown stale. The laughter and love she once experienced had faded into loneliness.

Judy tried everything to get her relationship with Mark back where it used to be. Desperate for his attention, she constantly told him how lonely she was. He couldn't understand why. Hoping for some meaningful communication, something to feel connected with him, she begged him to talk with her. He didn't know what to say. She tried ignoring him for days on end, hoping he would notice her silence and realize she was in pain. But he didn't. She struggled with the temptation to leave him and find someone—*anyone*—who would appreciate her. But she knew that wasn't an option.

Judy had been desperate like this before. It was at this point that she got out of a previous marriage. But Judy knew that God wanted her to stick this out. It just seemed impossible.

She began reading Proverbs 31 on a daily basis, telling herself that she needed to be the kind of wife who would draw her husband to her. She absorbed herself in marriage self-help books, Bible studies, fellowship with other Christian women. She made a career change and took some confidence-building steps in her life. But, she was still aching and alone.

Finally, Judy got on her knees and poured out her heart to God. She told him that the only thing that mattered was that she have a pure heart toward the Lord. She vowed to love Him with all her heart and focus on pleasing only Him. She immediately switched her focus from Mark to the Lord and what *He* could do for her. She concentrated not on Mark's shortcomings, but on how the Lord made up for them by holding her heart together and being her First Love. She quit thinking about how Mark saw her and concentrated only on how she could be right and acceptable in God's sight.

Then something began to happen. Judy gradually became a new woman. The frazzled 39-year-old with tear-swollen eyes began to glow with the vigor of a 25-year-old. Her whole demeanor took on a new radiance as she began to live like a woman truly loved and cherished. That's because she was. And she finally realized it. Within a couple of months, her husband began to notice that he had a new wife, as well.

"What happened?" I asked Judy one morning at church. "You seem so happy these days. Has Mark really made a turnaround or what?"

"No, not really," she smiled in her now-usual glow. "I'm learning to seek contentment from my relationship with the Lord."

Mark eventually became more loving toward her as her expectations upon him diminished. But was he suddenly able to meet her emotional needs? Not really. The difference was that Judy became so focused on the Lord that she really didn't notice what Mark was or wasn't doing anymore. She was taking her needs to the Only One who could meet them. And she was finding herself fulfilled, not feeling empty. She was happy. Mark was happy. And their marriage started to work again.

Judy had finally found the Only One who can satisfy.

THE SEARCH FOR SOMEONE

We all need *someone.* As women, we have a built-in desire for companionship, encouragement, tenderness, love. We desire to feel beautiful, accepted, and cherished. We long for someone with whom to share our hopes and dreams, our heart and our mind. We long for those things so much that, like Judy, we become frustrated—and sometimes desperate—when we don't get them.

Our needs, when it comes to love, are not wrong. God made us with those needs. It's interesting, however, that God didn't provide for those needs in the way we'd expect.

When our Creator made the first man, He saw that it wasn't good for him to be alone. He noticed Adam's needs for companionship, encouragement, help, and sexual compatibility. God responded to Adam's needs by creating a woman.[1] But it appears that God stopped there, doesn't it? I mean, He didn't go back and double check to see if this man he had already made was able to meet the complex needs of this creation called woman. Didn't He see, right off the bat, that Eve and all women after her would long for communication, intimacy, attentiveness, emotional support, a sense of value, and purpose? If He was aware of our needs, it seems He would've made our counterpart with more of a natural ability and desire to meet those needs. But ask any man today if communication, nurturing a relationship, and emotional intimacy are

_ite things to do" list and you'll find that
﹍l, seem to fall far short of meeting the emo-
﹍*tations* of women.

﹍t's not because God made a mistake. Our Creator
﹍e man in His own image and He made him perfect. Of
course, man sinned and is now no longer perfect. But to
point to that as the reason that women are unfulfilled,
would be to imply that God's plan of a man and woman's
perfect union went awry.

No, God had another plan. By instilling in the woman
certain desires for intimacy, communication, and emotional
fulfillment, He was reserving a place in her heart that only
He could fill. He was setting up a homing beacon within us
that would eventually lead us back to Him. As a result, we
are creatures of longing who will continue to search passionately for fulfillment, exhausting our relationships in the
process, until we eventually, like Judy, find the Source of
our Satisfaction.

LOOKING FOR LOVE IN ALL THE WRONG PLACES

Unfortunately, many of us start out looking in the
wrong place for our fulfillment. We depend on human relationships to bring us the kind of emotional intimacy and
fulfillment we're seeking. As children, we seek that love
and security from our parents. As we get older, we search
for fulfillment among our friends. Eventually, we look for
love and intimacy from the opposite sex. And we're convinced that fulfillment can only come from a person we can
touch and feel. After all, the Lord can't cuddle up with us in
front of the fire, take His hand and wipe away our tears,
bring us flowers to make us feel appreciated, say a lovely
thing to us to brighten our day, call us from work just to tell
us He loves us. No, the Lord doesn't perform those expressions of affection we've come to expect from "love." Or
does He?

In Psalm 139, I see a description of the Lord as One who knows us intimately (verses 1-6), who accepts us wholeheartedly—He actually planned our lives—(verses 13-18), and someone who wants to be in our presence so badly that He actually follows us everywhere we go (verses 7-12). He literally can't get enough of us. That is committed love. That is devotion. That, for me, is better than roses at the door or a call to say, "I love you." God pursues us with a love that is like nothing we've ever seen before.

If the Lord is the Perfect One, the Only One who can satisfy, why is it that we don't go to Him with our needs? Probably because we aren't convinced that He can meet us on an emotional level. We tend to see God as spiritual and only able to meet our needs for forgiveness, salvation, and peace of mind. Yet, our needs for love, tenderness, companionship, encouragement, and communication are needs that gnaw at our insides just as much as those seemingly deeper spiritual needs. Why, then, couldn't the Lord meet those, too?

Many women I've counseled complain that they just don't *feel* that God is there. They know in their heads that God is a source of comfort, the One who fulfills, and the One who can meet their needs. But they have a hard time moving that from their heads, where they know it, to their hearts, where they can *feel* it.

For instance, as women we need to feel loved, cherished, and appreciated not just for the things we do in our homes and for our families, but for who we are. We need to feel significant and important in our roles at work and home. We need to feel that someone somewhere is thinking about us and wanting to be with us. A woman I once counseled said that as long as her two sons loved and needed her, she had the strength and motivation to get out of bed everyday.

There are times I just need to be understood and loved, in spite of my failures. I need a loving look, a tender touch, a warm smile. During times when I'm down on myself, I need someone else to believe in me, encourage me, think the world of me. You may be a woman who just needs someone to talk to now and then. Or maybe you need a good listener who truly cares about what you're going through now and then. Statistics say we need so many hugs a day to be emotionally and physically healthy. I know I do. You may want to take a moment to think of some needs that you have that perhaps I haven't mentioned.

Now, do these needs that I mentioned (and some that you may have thought of) sound like something the Lord could meet? At first, it may not seem so. After all, how could a God in heaven, who is spiritual by nature, meet the physical and emotional needs of a human being here on earth?

Well, let's consider that by looking briefly at some of the characteristics of the Lord Jesus. (We'll look at each one in depth in the chapters that follow.)

- He accepts you as you are, regardless of your past.[2]
- He is faithful and will never leave you.[3]
- He knows your thoughts and intentions.[4]
- He is easy to approach.[5]
- He's the perfect friend.[6]
- He's an excellent communicator (and listener!).[7]
- He's got a great background and family.[8]
- He's easy to read—you can know exactly how to please Him.[9]
- He's a great encourager and He always has your best in mind.[10]

A LOVER LIKE NO ONE ELSE

In addition to those qualities, the Lord has some characteristics that set Him apart from any earthly love we could find:

He can read your heart and mind

I've heard some women say their husbands can look at them and know exactly what they're thinking. I envy them. To have a mind-reader husband would be quite nice. But for most of us, no one knows what we're thinking and feeling, until we try to express it in words, which often don't come out quite right. The Lord, however, can enter the private area of our minds and hearts—the part no one else can see—and know exactly what we're thinking and feeling. What's more, He goes to work in communicating His love to us in order to give us what we need.

David, the psalmist, prayed, "O LORD, you have searched me and you know me...you perceive my thoughts from afar...you are familiar with all my ways" (Psalm 139:1-3 NIV). David goes on to say that even before he speaks, the Lord knows what he is going to say. That is intimate knowledge—so intimate that David admits it is too wonderful for him to understand.

As a child, I always expected my mom to know what I was thinking, to know when to come in my room and comfort me when I was upset. And when she didn't, I became angry. I do the same thing to my husband today. So many times I want him to talk with me, so I leave clues that are, in my opinion, obvious. But my husband often has other things on his mind and doesn't pick up on my "hints." That angers me and makes me feel I'm not important enough for him to study and try to figure out.

God doesn't need the hints, though. He already knows the condition of my heart and mind. And because

He knows my thoughts, He understands me in a way no one else ever could. Better than a mother. Better than a husband. Better than a best friend. He knows me, literally, more than I know myself. And with all that intimate knowledge, He still loves me and accepts me. Now that's unconditional, unfathomable love.

He pursues us for a loving, intimate relationship

The same God who knew David and was intimately acquainted with all his ways knows each of us as well. And He wants to fellowship with us in an intimate way. In fact, He knows us so well and knows where we are at all times that He sticks to us like glue. We can't shake Him off.

As I mentioned before, Psalm 139:7-12 says, in short, that we can't go anywhere without Him being there. Imagine that! He loves us so much that He doesn't want to be separated from us. He wants to be our first love.

Jesus said in Luke 13:34, "Jerusalem, Jerusalem.... How often I wanted to gather your children together, just as a hen gathers her brood under her wings, and you would not have it!" Those words, spoken by a God who never changes to a people He came to save, ring true for us today. How often Jesus longs to do for us what He really came to do. In today's words, perhaps Jesus would've said, "Oh, lonely and weary woman. How often I wanted to gather you into my arms and love and comfort you, but you wouldn't have it. You continued to long for comfort from somebody else."

Not only do we long for somebody other than our Creator, but it's somebody our Creator knows is not able to meet our needs. We long for love and tenderness from our parents, our children, our friends, and our lovers. Yet all those people are human, and therefore sinners. They can't possibly give us perfectly fulfilling love like the Lord can.

Now I'm not saying we have no need for human relationships. God created marriage, family, and friendships so we could enjoy relationships here on earth. And it is God's design that our husbands, parents, children, and friends live with us in a harmonious way, adding to the joy and fullness of our lives. But God wants to be the *ultimate* relationship in our life, the One from whom we derive our greatest satisfaction, the One whose love we crave, the One who steals our heart away.

We long for comfort and care from anyone else whom we can touch and hold. Yet when we depend on other people, the Bible says in Jeremiah 17:5-6, we become like brittle bushes in the desert—empty, dried-out, longing for refreshment, dying for love. And a bush in the desert is unable to receive the nourishment it needs to grow and bloom. Contrast that idea with Psalm 65:9-11, which says "the stream of God is full of water" and His "paths drip with fatness." When we go to Him for refreshment (and love), His stream doesn't run dry; there's always enough to satisfy. And when we choose His path to fulfillment, we won't find ourselves lost and empty.

WE HAVE A HOLY HUSBAND

Not only does the Lord pursue us, but regardless of our response He still considers Himself our husband. That's right—we have a "holy Husband."

Isaiah 54:5 says, "For your husband is your Maker, whose name is the LORD of Hosts." While those words were literally spoken to the nation of Israel, through the prophet Isaiah, we can glean truth and meaning from them today. Just as God pursued the nation of Israel and wanted her all for Himself, wanted to be her loving and faithful husband, so the Lord today pursues us as a husband madly in love.

Throughout the Bible, God uses the illustration of a bridegroom seeking his bride to describe His desired relationship with His chosen ones. That kind of pursuing, that kind of love, makes Him more than just a Supreme Being whom we thank before meals and sing and pray to on Sunday. That makes Him a God who is intimately acquainted with us. He is ready for the commitment. Are *you*?

When you take part in that intimacy He offers, you can, like Judy, begin to live like a woman who is truly loved and cherished. And your longings will find fulfillment in the Only One who can satisfy.

RESPONDING TO HIS INVITATION

If the Lord is capable of meeting all your needs, why don't you *feel* like He's doing it? Well, the Lord's relationship with us is no different than any other kind of relationship in that it takes two people to make it work. If God is doing the calling, the pursuing, the initiating and you are not responding, that's as far as it will go. You can know in your head that He wants a relationship with you, but until you actually respond with your heart and say "I do," you won't be able to experience it.

Jeremiah 29:13 says, "You will seek Me and find Me, when you search for Me with all your heart." Are you searching for Him, literally, with *all your heart*? Is intimacy with Him the one thing you desire more than anything else? If so, God's Word promises you will find it.

In any relationship, intimacy and trust grow as we spend time with one another. As we become vulnerable with one another. As we learn to love and grow and trust each other. If your relationship with Christ, at this point, consists only of a quick greeting and request each day, it needs more.

First, you must accept His invitation of love

If you have never had a personal relationship with Jesus, this is how you get started. According to the Bible, all of us have sinned (Romans 3:23) and therefore cannot live in the presence of a Holy God and so we face death as God's required judgment for our sin. But Jesus, God's Son, came to earth to live a sinless life and die a sacrificial death, thereby doing what we couldn't and appeasing God's sense of justice. Jesus' death bridged the gap between our sinfulness and God's holiness and so now, through faith in Jesus and His atoning death for us, we can have a relationship with God. God requires only that we admit we are hopeless without Him and we desire to turn from our dependence on self and others and live according to the plan that He has for us. By accepting God's invitation of love—the salvation He provided through His Son, Jesus—we begin trusting Him for *eternal life.*

You must then get to know Him, by spending time with Him

In any relationship, we must spend time with another person before we know if we really want to stay together. The more time you spend with God—through prayer and through the reading of His Word—the more you learn about Him. And the more you get to know Him, the more you will want to stay within His embrace. Getting to know Him involves learning what He loves and what He hates, what pleases Him and what grieves His heart. You can know what He wants *from* you and *for* you by spending time reading His Word and communicating with Him in prayer. That's trusting Him with your *everyday life.*

Finally, you must deepen your intimacy with Him by making Him your First Love

It's great to date. But who wants to date forever? When you finally make the decision to get serious with that someone, then the ball gets rolling. It's the same way in your relationship with the Lord. We can read His Word and pray 'til we're blue in the face, but until we make the decision to get serious with God, we're still just dating and testing the waters. It's the dating stage where many Christians stop. They trust God for *eternal* life, by letting Him save their souls and take them to heaven. But they don't trust Him in their *everyday* life, by letting Him direct their hearts and lives on a daily basis. When we leave Him out of our daily life, we miss one of the most rewarding aspects of trusting Him—seeing Him in action as He involves Himself in the daily details of our lives.

Getting serious with Him means sharing more and more of your life with Him and becoming exclusive in your affection for Him. It means no one else competes with Him in your heart. Jesus said He came so we can have life more abundantly (John 10:10). That means He didn't just come to give us eternal life. He came to give us a fulfilled life here on earth, as well. An abundant life for a woman is a fulfilled life, a life of joy, meaning, purpose, satisfaction, love. When we make Jesus our First Love, above everyone else, we experience an intimacy and joy we never knew before. And we begin trusting Him with our *emotional life*.

There are three things to keep in mind in order to make Him your First Love and deepen your intimacy with Him:

- **Tell Him first.** Tell Him what's on your heart, what you need, what you're excited about, what went wrong. When things happen in your life, the first person you go to with the news is often the most important person in your life. Affirm to the Lord that He is the most important person in your life by letting Him be the first one you talk to in the morning, the last one you speak with at night.

- **Take Him seriously.** In every relationship there are consequences to messing up. By not consulting with your loved one before making an important decision or by disregarding his views on something and doing it anyway, you put a relationship in jeopardy. Take the Lord and His commands seriously. Find out what He loves and cling to it. Know what He hates and avoid it at all costs. Make every decision in life one that revolves around and considers your love and respect for Him. In all your ways acknowledge Him and your relationship will move along smoothly (Proverbs 3:6).

- **Trust Him fully.** There will be times when God asks something of you or allows something to happen that you cannot understand. That's where your trust comes in. Trusting Him fully means taking your greatest fears (the death of your child or husband? the loss of your dreams? a diagnosis of cancer?) and placing them at His feet, acknowledging that God is in control of your life and you will trust Him no matter what pain may come your way to ultimately shape you for His purposes.

Because trusting God fully is so difficult to do, I want to explain it a little more, using an example from my own life.

As I was growing up, my greatest fear was that my parents would divorce. Many times, as a child, I would lie awake in bed, imagining the pain and turmoil if my parents were to separate and asking God to cement my commitment to Him so that I would never walk away from Him no matter how angry or hurt I might feel.

I was 19 years old and working at a summer job out of state when I got the dreaded phone call from home: My parents had split up—after 22 years of marriage—and the home I left would not be the same when I returned.

As I hung up the phone, I felt the storm blow in. Waves of anger, hurt, and disappointment welled up inside of me and my boat was rocking back and forth. I realized at that moment that I had a choice: I could jump ship and drown. Or I could trust that my Anchor would hold and the storm would pass.

I chose to trust in my Anchor, the One whose promises I learned as a child, the One who knew that my parents would one day take this course, the One who could turn all things—even the bad things—into good for my life. And I discovered over the next several months that my Anchor held. The pain *was* bearable. His comfort and sustaining power *was* enough. And the Lord *did* use the situation for good in my life by drawing me closer to Him during my time of turmoil.

Trusting Him fully is setting your anchor of trust deep with the Lord, *before* disaster strikes, so that when sudden seasons of change, uncertainty, pain or loss blow into your life, you don't drift away, jump ship, or sink.

Many women struggle with fears, worries, and the constant "what if?" Take these fears and "what ifs" to the Lord, asking Him to give you a trust now that if and when those things come, you'll be able to stand firm. Just like in a marriage or a close friendship, intimacy with God can never fully develop if absolute trust is not present. When we do finally learn to love Him, and therefore trust Him fully, we will be able to experience the truth of 1 John 4:18: "...perfect love casts out fear." Perfect love means to trust God fully. And trusting Him fully means "no fear."

IT'S YOUR CHOICE

God has invited you to join him in a perfect love relationship. But it's up to you to respond. In any marriage or friendship, we can't expect it to thrive if we fail to communicate, don't respond to what the other person asks of us, and so on. When we know God and what pleases Him, we can concentrate on being what *He wants* in a relationship—someone who loves Him back, desires to please Him, and lives in harmony with Him. As you learn more about the qualities and character of your new Lover (throughout the rest of this book), you will naturally want to grow closer to Him. And as you two grow together and go the distance, you will discover how satisfying and fulfilling intimacy with God can be.

May it be your goal from this point forward to never give God the opportunity to say to you, "Oh lonely woman. How often I wanted to gather you in My arms, but you would not have it!" Be the woman, instead, who anxiously runs into His open arms and nestles into the love that awaits you.

Steps for Starting Out

By grabbing hold of the Only One who can satisfy and making Him your First Love, you are off to a great start in finding true love and the intimacy that will meet your greatest needs and fulfill your deepest hunger. Go through these steps and, as you do, you will get another step closer to understanding your Lover's heart.

1. If you have never accepted God's invitation of love through a personal relationship with Jesus, do so now by confessing to Him that you have sought fulfillment elsewhere in life and asking Him to enter your life and be the Captain of your heart. Thank Him for saving you from your sin and for giving you eternal life. Ask Him to be a part of your everyday life by guiding you and directing you according to His will. Vow to do your part in the relationship by being obedient to His Word and responding to His love in commitment to only Him. (Make sure you tell someone of your new commitment, particularly someone who will support and encourage you in this exciting new step!)

If you have already accepted God's invitation of love, take time now to recommit yourself to the Only One who satisfies. Write a letter to Him expressing your newfound commitment to Him alone.

2. Write out a plan for spending intimate time with the Lord each day. (Include the time you will set aside, the place you will go, and what you will do during that time—read through the Psalms, go through a Bible study book, begin a prayer and meditation journal, and so on.)

Time _____

Place _____

Plan _____

3. Think of ways you can make the Lord your First Love in your everyday life. (I'll give you some ideas to get you started. Feel free to add several more if you'd like and commit to them throughout the week.)

- Today I will "do lunch" with the Lord by spending my lunch hour thinking of Him, reading some of His promises, and letting Him know how much I love Him.
- I will take my expectations, concerns, disappointments and "breaking news" to the Lord first this week, just to remind Him and myself that He is the most important one in my life.
- I will re-examine my weekly schedule and priorities to make sure nothing is coming between my time with the Lord, with studying His Word, with worshiping Him, with fellowshiping with His people.

- _____
  _____

- _____
  _____

- _____
  _____

- _____
  _____

2
Knowing He Accepts Me

I grew up believing I had to earn my father's love. When I received good grades, held coveted positions, or earned honors or awards, my dad was proud. And when he felt proud, I felt loved. I don't remember my dad expressing affection toward me verbally, except when he would say, "I'm proud of you, Ceenee." Because I interpreted that as, "I love you, Cindi," I became an overachiever. My life was focused on making Dad proud and feeling acceptable in his sight.

I vividly remember the day I felt Dad's love withdrawn. I was a sophomore in high school and brought home my first "B" on my report card—in geometry. My father hit the roof! He immediately drove down to the school and blamed my teacher for not teaching me adequately and for having the nerve to give his daughter anything less than an "A." In his sadly twisted way, Dad was trying to express that he loved me by insisting that I only be given the best grades. But at the same time, I felt I had blown it in his eyes, and I was no longer accepted by him.

Three years later, I brought home my first speeding ticket. Dad was furious and accused me of being irresponsible and unworthy of being his daughter. It became a crucial point in our relationship. I feared his anger and what he might do to me. Shortly afterward I moved out of my parents' house and into an apartment with my sister. I feared ever disappointing *anyone* again. And it took me a long time to feel accepted again by my father.

Because of the work of the Holy Spirit, my father is a different person today. He recognizes my humanity and admits he has made many mistakes. I am now confident that he loves me for who I am, not what I've done and will continue to do. But my perception of unconditional love—whether from my husband or my heavenly Father or anyone else—had already been shaped.

DEALING WITH OUR FEARS

It's difficult for me to understand that my Heavenly Father loves me for who I am, not what I've done and will do. And to this day, when I disappoint the Lord with a heart that isn't right or sin that should've been avoided, I still fight those thoughts in the back of my mind—that I am no longer accepted by Him and that He doesn't love me anymore.

My insecurities about being accepted continued into my marriage relationship. In the first few years of my marriage I was terribly fearful that if my husband discovered who I *really* was, he wouldn't want me anymore. When we married, he was under the impression that I had a gentle, quiet spirit and that I was soft-spoken, well-refined, and emotionally all-together. He soon found out I was a talker and that I could get quite loud, especially around members of my family. He discovered I had a bad habit of interrupting people and I was much more emotionally fragile than he'd ever imagined. About the same time he discovered the *real* me, I was finding out that he wasn't the stellar communicator I thought he was. While I had grown up in a family in which everyone talked at once and freely expressed how they felt, he grew up in a silent home, where he was taught to stuff his feelings deep inside and never talk about them. After years of lashing out at him for not opening up and talking to me, he finally admitted the ugly truth: He never talks to me because he can't get a word in edgewise! He would *start* talking, he said, if I could *stop* talking. How humiliating! And, because of my fears of not being accepted, how very threatening!

The most difficult task for both of us in our marriage has been accepting each other's flaws. I didn't want to accept that my husband may never be the communicator I thought he was when we married. But by accepting that as a part of the complete package that is him, it teaches me to love him a little more unconditionally. And by his accepting the fact that I may never have the quiet and gentle composure he believed me to have when we married, he shows me how very deeply he must love me.

Our longing for acceptance is often just as strong as our fear of rejection. So we tend to hide the parts about us that we fear will not be accepted in order to feel loved and avoid rejection. Sometimes it's our bad habits, deeply ingrained in us since childhood, that we hide from others, as Hugh and I tried to do. But sometimes it's stuff much deeper than that...deep, dark secrets of our past that we hope no one will find out.

WHAT ABOUT OUR PAST?

Everyone goes into a relationship with baggage. Some baggage is a little easier to sort through than others. Shortly after I was married, I made the mistake of going through one of my husband's bags that would have been better left alone. But, by discovering some painful things in his past, I learned something more about acceptance.

My husband had a night job, which meant he would return home late. One evening as I was waiting for him to come home, I found his old high school yearbook and began flipping through the pages. I knew my husband had had a girlfriend in high school before he became a Christian. And he had leveled with me about his mistakes, in general, before he began walking with the Lord. But I was curious about the details. Although I was convicted in my heart not to delve into this matter, because it was a relationship prior to his knowing the Lord, I also felt I had a right to know more.

I didn't even know the girl's name, but it didn't take me long to figure out which signature in his yearbook was hers. I read what she wrote and felt sick to my stomach. I would have been better off not reading about the details and things she implied on that page.

That night, when my husband got home and inquired about my mood, I mentioned briefly that I had found his yearbook and read through it. He wasn't offended at my invasion of his privacy, as I expected him to be. He, instead, was hurt...at having to be reminded of his past and see me hurt by it as well. After a long time, he broke the silence.

"I did a lot of dumb things before I gave my life to the Lord," he admitted to me, with tears in his eyes. "And I'm not proud of them. I don't want to think about the way I used to live. That's not me anymore. I'm a different person now in God's eyes."

I realized then that acceptance means love without condition, without certain expectations of the past or the future. It is a decision to love no matter what happened yesterday and no matter what happens tomorrow. By bringing up my husband's past, I had hurt him deeply. God forgave my husband's sin and threw away his past when he became saved. Who was I to bring this up again when God had wiped his slate clean? That night, I decided I would spend the rest of my life trying to show my husband how very much I love him for *who* he is, not for what he's done or what he will do. And by trying to do that through the years, I've learned how precious it is not only to be fully accepted myself, but to fully accept another person regardless of their past, present, or future.

WHAT ARE YOU HIDING?

Whether it's something about our personality or something buried in our past, many women enter relationships hoping the other person will never know the deep, dark secrets they hide. Past relationships or reputations, abortions or addictions...the list abounds of things we would rather not expose about ourselves for fear of not being accepted.

Some of us never go beyond a certain point in relationships, fearing that if we become too close to a person, we will eventually be hurt because they might not accept us for who we really are.

No matter how you look at it, knowing we are accepted is crucial to feeling secure and loved in any relationship.

When my mother entered her second marriage, my brothers and sister and I wondered if her new husband knew what he was getting into. Hadn't he ever seen her when she completely lost it? What would happen the first time, or after several times, that she freaked out about something minor? Amazingly to us, however, my mother and her husband have been married nearly 15 years and plan to remain so until one of them leaves this earth. Don, my step-dad, knows all about Mom's "freak outs." He's seen several of them occur when she's been under stress or out of the Word. Yet he has accepted that as part of the package. He has accepted her in spite of the things about her that are unattractive. He took the good with the not-so-good. That is unconditional love.

JESUS KNEW THE ART OF ACCEPTANCE

Jesus feels the same way about us. When Jesus was passing through a town called Samaria, He stopped near a well to have a conversation with a woman—a woman with a worldly reputation. He struck up the conversation by asking her to draw some water for Him. Not only was this woman of a nationality that Jesus' people, the Jews, found offensive, but she was a sinner, one that you'd think God would find offensive. Jesus crossed a cultural barrier by speaking to this woman on a deserted road. But regardless of this woman's nationality, sex, and troubled past, Jesus talked with her and asked her for some water.

The woman hesitated. *If he knew the kind of woman I was, he wouldn't be talking to me*, she must have thought.

Jesus knew what she was thinking. "Where's your husband?" He asked.

"I don't have one," she replied, perhaps a bit flustered.

She *didn't* have a husband—at least not at the moment. She'd been through quite a few husbands, however. And she was now living with a man who wasn't her husband. Why hadn't he married her? Because of her reputation? Because she was afraid to tell the latest man her true story? All we know is that she wasn't completely honest with Jesus when He asked if she was married. Most likely, she didn't want to talk about it.

Yet Jesus knew. And despite this woman's past, He offered her living water.[1]

He offers us the same. In addition to the life-giving forgiveness of our past, He offers us the water of relief and refreshment in a life in which we no longer have to keep things hidden. We can be up-front with Him and it will not affect His love for us one bit.

FINDING OUR ACCEPTANCE

There is only one way we become acceptable to God and that is when we have accepted His Son, Jesus Christ, and are depending on Him for our salvation. Jesus, God's obedient Son, is holy and perfect in God's eyes. And when we are trusting in Jesus, we become holy and perfect as well, because He represents us and His righteousness becomes ours.[2] Once we have repented of our sin and trusted in Jesus for salvation, there is nothing we can do to be "unaccepted" in God's eyes.

Now, that's a wonderful concept. That means that if I mess up, I'm still okay with Him. If I make a wrong choice and push the line with Him, I may have consequences to bear because of my actions, but I am still loved. That means I can be completely honest with Him without any fear that He might cast me away.

When was the last time you told the Lord, your Heavenly Husband, how you were really feeling? Have you ever tried sharing with Him the things you refuse to tell anyone else? If not, draw it out for Him. By doing this, you will lift a burden that you've been carrying far too long.

In Matthew 11:28-30, Jesus told us to come to Him with our burdens and He'll lighten our load. That means we can tell Him what's on our mind. We can unload the things we're afraid to tell anyone else and we can experience the relief of no longer having to carry that burden alone. We can draw out for Him what is buried deep in our hearts and He will give us the water of relief and refreshment in return.

ASSESSING YOUR FEARS

Some of the women I've counseled have been afraid to admit to their husbands their previous sexual relationships. One woman I know has buried the guilt of past abortions deep in her heart and mind, unwilling to talk about it to her husband, family, or friends, for fear of being judged and condemned by them. Other women I've counseled have hidden a past of sexual molestation by family members, feeling they will be looked at differently if their past is revealed.

Take a moment to think about some things in your past that you feel embarrassed or ashamed about—things about yourself that you wouldn't necessarily want others to know. Do you have *anyone* in your life that you can reveal these things to without fearing rejection?

Now, let's look at how the Lord views the things that linger in our past.

He considers them in the past and no longer relevant

The Bible says anyone who has a relationship with Christ is just like a new person. The past is forgotten and everything is new again (2 Corinthians 5:17). That means any sin or mistake we make prior to knowing God is erased from our history. We get a clean slate when we come to Him.

He doesn't let our past mistakes affect how we look in His eyes

Isaiah 1:18 says, "'Come now, and let us reason together,' says the Lord, 'Though your sins are as scarlet, they will be as white as snow; though they are red like crimson, they will be like wool.'" Again, He loves us for who we are, not what we do and don't do.

He chooses to forget our mistakes and He never keeps an account

In Isaiah 43:25 God says, "I, even I, am the one who wipes out your transgressions for My own sake; and I will not remember your sins." A big part of being accepted is being assured of the fact that our past won't be brought up time after time. The Lord assures us that things we've repented of are behind us and will never have to haunt us again.[3] In Psalm 103:12, David eloquently describes this freedom from our mistakes: "As far as the east is from the west, so far has He removed our transgressions from us."

When we come to Christ and He cleans our slate, we get a new start. He still knows who we are and where we came from. But He doesn't hold that against us. Sometimes I think He considers it a delightful challenge to see how much He can transform us into His likeness and how far He can take us in our new life with Him (see 1 Corinthians 1:26-31).

In the first chapter of this book we looked at how God knows us intimately and still loves us. Psalm 139, which tells of the Lord's intimate knowledge of us, reminds us that He formed us in the womb and saw our unformed bodies and already ordained for us the number of days we would live before we had even been born.[4] That tells us that He not only knows our past, but He planned us out, meaning He had a hand in how we came about and what we were before we came to know Him. With that in mind, of course He accepts us so willingly. We're His creation, His special project that has come back to Him after a run on our own. And we didn't even have to prove ourselves to Him so He would take us back.

Romans 5:8 says, "God demonstrates His own love toward us, in that *while we were yet sinners*, Christ died for us" (emphasis added). We didn't even have to clean up our act before He decided He would save us. Because there was nothing we could do to earn His love, there's nothing we can do to lose it. Face it, my friend: You are accepted in the beloved.

ACCEPTED, BUT NOT EXCUSED

It's important for us to know that although we are accepted by God, we are not excused for the things that He clearly disapproves of. God grieves at our sin. But He loves us as individuals.

I am grieved when my husband doesn't communicate. But I accept that it's difficult for him and therefore I try to be patient in working with him in this area of vulnerability. I was grieved at discovering things about my husband's past, but I didn't let it affect how I love him today. And, although I accept him regardless of his past, there are certain things I would not accept today if he were to revert back to the person he used to be.

When we are forgiven by God and accepted into His family, we are not given a license to continue sinning.[5] When we know something is wrong and we do it anyway, it is never acceptable to God. It is forgivable, when we are truly sorry for it. But His grace and forgiveness never give us a go-ahead to continue in sinful behavior. Sometimes coming to God with something that we are ashamed of or struggling with involves confrontation—His Spirit convicting us to get the help we need and to make the necessary changes in our lives.

When Jesus talked to the Samaritan woman, He accepted her, but He did not excuse her lifestyle. Later, when Jesus came upon a woman accused of adultery, He refused to condemn her. But He didn't excuse her actions. In fact, He told her "From now on sin no more."[6] Again, our continued forgiveness is contingent upon our willingness to make the desired changes.

If you are struggling with a pattern of life that is destructive (dishonesty, compulsive behavior, substance abuse, addictions, habitual sin, and so on) God's desire for you is to get the help you need. Confess this problem to the Lord and then talk to a pastor or Christian counselor who can direct you, if possible, to a biblically based recovery program, support group, or accountability relationship. Depend on the Lord and the accountability group He leads you to in order to make a turnaround. Sometimes our acceptance depends greatly on our sincerity and desire to change. God knows our hearts. He knows when we truly desire forgiveness and change, and when we are just continuing to take advantage of grace.

When we truly desire acceptance in God's eyes, we can pray, as David did:

> *Search me, O God, and know my heart;*
> *Try me and know my anxious thoughts;*
> *And see if there be any hurtful way in me,*
> *And lead me in the everlasting way.*[7]

ACCEPTING THE TRUTH

No matter what is in our past, no matter what we may be struggling with in our present, God loves and accepts us like no other. When we realize how generously God has accepted us, it not only deepens our trust and intimacy with Him, but it enables us to more generously accept others, bringing harmony to our earthly relationships. Remember, since you didn't earn this acceptance from God (it was given to you freely), you can't lose it, either. His acceptance of you was there before the beginning of time and it will be there on into eternity. Living in the light of this acceptance can make you a confident, capable woman of God as you realize that you are His creation, His pride and joy, His much-loved bride. So take heart, my friend, and stand tall. You and I are accepted by our Beloved.

Steps to Feeling Accepted

As you gain a greater understanding of God's unconditional love and acceptance, your heart will be inclined to
draw closer to His. Here are a few steps to help you let go
of any baggage that is keeping you from fully understanding and embracing the Lord's love and acceptance of you:

1. Perhaps you're struggling in a relationship where
you don't feel accepted. Pour your heart out to God right
now, letting Him know your fears and insecurities, and
claim His acceptance and unconditional love.

2. Perhaps you're having difficulty accepting someone
else. If so, ask the Lord to give you the wisdom to know
which behaviors and characteristics you need to accept and
which you need to lovingly confront. Pray about this now.
Determine an action to show your acceptance to another.

3. Is there something in your life that you know God
does *not* accept (although His love for you still prevails)?
Confess this to the Lord. Thank Him for His forgiveness.
Determine to live in His strength without repeating the
mistakes of the past. (You may want to find a more mature
believer to talk with or a fellowship group that deals with
this issue and provides accountability.) Talk with a pastor
or trusted Christian friend about your desire to come clean
in this area.

3
Realizing He'll Never Leave

I grew up with a mother who would often leave. After an argument with my father, she would run out the door, slam it behind her, get into her car, and race out of the driveway, screeching the tires as she left. Sometimes she was gone for a few hours. Sometimes for a few days. We never knew *when* she would come back. We just always hoped she *would*.

Mom used to say it was good for her to leave us and our father. It helped her deal with us better. And it made her miss us and love us more when she returned. "You need time away from the people you love in order to love them better," she would say. Naturally, I grew up believing that people who loved me would leave.

One day Mom finally left for good. While I was working at a Christian Conference Center in another state, Mom took my two younger brothers and moved to a mountain community 60 miles southeast of our home. She called to inform me she had left and she wouldn't be there when I got home. She wouldn't say where she was; she said she needed her time away and wasn't ready to be found.

At the same time Mom left, I was involved in my first serious relationship with a young man I believed I would someday marry. He, too, would leave the relationship often.

Sometimes it was because he discovered something about me he wasn't sure he wanted to put up with. Other times he wanted to re-evaluate the relationship to see if he really wanted it to continue. And sometimes he just wanted to see if there was someone out there who was more exciting than me. Although his leaving the relationship physically and emotionally was painful to me, I was beginning to get used to it. Each time he left, I told myself that he would return and love me a little bit more. After all, people who really loved me had to leave me.

Unfortunately, I learned a lie. And by God's grace my eyes were opened to the truth about love and leaving when I met the man I eventually married. Hugh, a Bible student in his first dating relationship since he was saved, told me that he wasn't the type who would ever ask for "time away."

"Why?" I asked, thinking maybe he didn't love me.

"*God* never wants time away from you, Cindi," he told me. "So neither will I."

God is our perfect role model in relationships. He shows us how to love one another, first and foremost by how He loves us. And the single most important aspect of His love is that He will never leave. Love does *not* mean leaving. Love means sticking it out.

LOVE THAT NEVER LEAVES

In the Bible, God tells us He will never leave us nor desert us. But He doesn't stop there. He takes it a step further by telling us He will never let *us* get away from Him. In Psalm 139, which we looked at earlier, God tells us He will not only never leave us, but He literally follows us around. There's nowhere we can go to get away from Him. We couldn't lose Him if we tried.

There are times when we may think He has left, but His Word promises He is still there. In Psalm 77, Asaph wondered aloud if God had deserted him. His circumstances and his loneliness told him he was alone, that God had forsaken His promise and had abandoned him. But then, in an eye-opening phrase, he admitted it was his own perception that had made him think God had left him.

"It is my grief, that the right hand of the Most High has changed," Asaph said in Psalm 77:10. Wisely, he knew his feelings had distorted the truth of God's character. Our God is a God who never leaves. And if we feel He has, our feelings have led us from the truth.

Asaph then began to see God's presence all around him. He talked of seeing God in nature: in the waters, the clouds that poured forth rain, the lightning that flashed across the sky, and in the thunderous boom from the heavens. Then Asaph declared something that we can all relate to if we understand the big picture. "Thy way was in the sea and Thy paths in the mighty waters, and *Thy footprints may not be known.*"[1]

During those times that we believe God is not around, His way is "in the sea" where footprints are not seen. (Have you ever tried to make a footprint under the water?) God sometimes does the unimaginable, like parting the seas to bring His people through on dry land. Sometimes He allows us a time of loneliness or silence while He is doing something great. But He assures us He is right there with us, even though His footprints aren't seen. God reaffirms this concept to us in Isaiah 43:2 when He promises us He will be *with us* through the waters, through the fire, through whatever comes our way. That means we don't have to worry about Him running out on us when times get tough. In fact, those are the times He sticks the closest to us.

LOVE THAT CAN'T BE REMOVED

Romans 8:38-39 says that *nothing* will be able to separate us from Christ and His intense love for us. Nothing! Not angelic nor demonic forces, not death, not things in this world nor things in the world to come. We can add to that list and say that not even our own decisions to love someone else *more* than God can keep His loving presence from us. He is determined and jealous in His love for us (Exodus 20:5) and a determined and jealous lover will not let the object of His affection out of His sight. So not only will God never leave us, His love will never take leave of us, either.

LOVE THAT INDWELLS US

Not only is the Lord always with us, but He actually *holds* us. Psalm 18:35 says, "Thou hast...given me the shield of Thy salvation, and *Thy right hand upholds me*" (emphasis added). Again in Psalm 63:8 we are told that as we cling to the Lord, His "right hand upholds [us]."

Isn't it great to know that God's promise to always be with us doesn't merely mean that His presence is around us like swirling air? It means He is holding us. And furthermore, it means that He dwells *within us*, through the power of the Holy Spirit, when we become His by accepting Him as our Savior. Imagine that! A Lover who dwells within us at every moment.

In Psalm 132:13 we are told, "The LORD has chosen Zion; He has desired it for His habitation." Just as the Lord has chosen Zion (Jerusalem) for His dwelling place, He has chosen *my heart* and *your heart* in which to dwell. The Lord goes on to say, (verse 14) "This is My resting place forever; here I will dwell, for I have desired it" (verse 14). God does not dwell within us out of compulsion or obligation. He dwells within us out of His *desire*. Why would God ever leave the place where He most wants to be? That's consistency. That's dependability. That's security.

THE "LEAVING" LIFESTYLE

Security like that in a love relationship is difficult to fathom. The headlines that sell women's magazines prey on the insecurities that women feel today. With so much emphasis on beauty, youth, and perfection, we, as women, live in constant fear that someone will leave us for someone better. I did. And had I not met a man who set me straight about God's love for me and His intention for how I should be loved, I might still be drifting in the sea of insecurity, feeling lost and alone.

Sometimes it's difficult to break out of the mindset that those who love us will leave. Why wouldn't it be? In our society, if we don't like our telephone company, we find another. If our bank doesn't provide enough free services, we find another. If we don't like our job, or our church, or our school, or our neighborhood, we simply move on and find one we like better. Sadly, this mentality exists in relationships, too. Most women, at one time or another, feel haunted by the statistics that nearly one in two marriages end in divorce. Songs tell us nothing lasts forever. Movies show us men who leave. And we all know a couple who appeared to be stable and then one or the other got up and left. How can we not be affected by the insecurity that our loved ones will do the same?

Well, rest assured, you who long for security in your relationship. You have it in the Lord!

REJECTED, BUT NOT FORSAKEN

Hagar was an Egyptian woman. A maid in the house of a millionaire. But she was also a victim of a scheme for Sarah and Abraham to attain a child of their own. Using Hagar's ability—her fertility and her body—to get what they wanted, Sarah and Abraham forced their maid to sleep in her master's bed in order to conceive a child. When the plan worked and Hagar became pregnant, she figured she would be the mother of the long-promised heir and that had to mean a ticket to a better life. But things backfired. Sarah instead hated Hagar and abused her. So Hagar ran away. Feeling lost, hurt, and alone,

Hagar didn't even bother calling upon the Lord. But she didn't have to. *He* called on her.

"Where are you going?" the Lord asked, gently, when He found Hagar sitting alone by a well with nowhere to go. When Hagar explained her difficult situation, God assured her He was still there. He told her He had a plan for her and her unborn child, and He instructed her to return to her home. He would take care of her. Hagar may have been rejected by the woman she considered her closest friend and by the only man she had ever been physically close to. But God hadn't rejected her. He was still there. He still loved her. Convinced of that, Hagar had the strength to return home and carry on. She had found her security. And her security was that the Lord would never leave her.[2]

FACING YOUR FEARS

What lurks at the center of *your* insecurity? A father who left when you were young? A fiancée or husband who changed his mind? A long list of relationships that didn't work out? A friend who disappointed you once you began to trust her?

Think about the things that would make you feel secure in your present relationship. How about always knowing where that person was and that he or she was thinking about you? How about always being within arm's reach of the person? How about a perfect track record of trust and reliability?

A neighbor of mine met her husband through an extramarital affair. Her husband left his first wife to marry her. Now her fear is that her husband will leave her for the next woman he's attracted to! Her insecurity is very real ...and understandable.

A few years ago when my toddler-aged daughter and I took a train up north to see my father for a few days, a 19-year-old girl I met seemed surprised I would leave my husband at home alone. "What if he sees someone else while you're gone?" she cringed. "I would never give my man a chance to be alone for a few days," she hissed with a look of skepticism. Her fear and insecurity was written all over her face. What she must have experienced at such a young age to be so incapable of trusting anyone!

But God is not like people who have disappointed us and let us down. We talked about His promise to never leave us or desert us, His determination to stick close to us, His way of *indwelling* us. Considering all that you know about Him and His love, couldn't He be the One to fill the insecurities in your life and make you feel safe and secure?

Perhaps before answering that, you should consider a few more things about your heavenly Husband.

SHEPHERD OF YOUR HEART

David the psalmist, who spent his teenage years herding sheep, likens the Lord to a Good Shepherd who lovingly cares for His sheep (Psalm 23). Interestingly, Jesus compared Himself to a Shepherd, too, indicating that He was willing to ward off wolves so His flock would be protected[3] or leave a whole flock to search for one lost sheep who needed to be brought back to the fold.[4] The fact that Jesus compared Himself to a Shepherd must mean that we are a lot like sheep—timid, frail, sometimes wandering where we shouldn't, often in danger of wolves. Even those of us who like to think of ourselves as independent still have times when we long for our "shepherd"—or "prince"—to come rescue us.

As the Good Shepherd, Jesus provides all that His sheep need to feel safe and secure, physically, spiritually, and emotionally. In the verses of the twenty-third Psalm, we can see the tender ways He shepherds our hearts:

He takes care of all my needs

Only recently have I realized what it means to "not be in want." When the Lord provides all I need—physically, emotionally, and spiritually—there is little more I could possibly want. We are truly content when we let Him be the faithful Shepherd and provide all our needs. When we can rest securely in Him like lambs in the arms of a shepherd, we often find He provides our *wants* as well.

He makes me stop and rest when He knows I need it

The Lord knows when I'm tired of trying, weary of crying, burned out, and bitter. So He leads me to a quiet place to rest so I can continue on. Sometimes we perceive this as God putting us on hold, when in fact He is forcing us to stop and rest for the journey that lies ahead. Often during those silent times of frustration when we claim "God isn't here anymore" He may actually be remaining quiet so we can get our needed rest.

He leads me beside "quiet waters," providing nourishment, peace, and tranquility

Like sheep, we all need water along the way—to revive us, restore us, and keep us going. But God doesn't just leave us to find it on our own. He *leads* us to the calm waters that will soothe our soul. His water of refreshment is His Word, which beckons to us. His peace and tranquility fill our soul when we're troubled. He's aware of our frame, that we are like dust, easily scattered if we don't get our share of "quiet waters."

He leads me along the right path so I'll avoid danger and stay out of trouble

God knows we are happiest when we're living right (Psalm 119:1). So He doesn't just set us loose to wander where we may. He leads and directs us along the path that is safest for us. Psalm 85:13 tells us, "Righteousness will go before Him, and will make His footsteps into a way." The King James Version puts it this way: "[He] shall set us in the way of his steps." When He guides, He actually walks before me, making sure I'm going on a safe path, an obedient path right behind Him, following His lead. I can follow happily, knowing my steps are stable and secure.

Following in His steps will also bring joy to my heart. Psalm 84:11 says the Lord "will make known to me the path of life; In [His] presence is fullness of joy; in [His] right hand there are pleasures forever." By leading us along His path of righteousness, our Shepherd is ensuring that we enjoy the journey and get as much out of it as we can. His path is not only secure, but pleasurable.

He comforts me through valleys of darkness

When I encounter times of uncertainty, I have the security of knowing my Shepherd is right there, leading the way. His staff reaches around my neck and pulls me to Him now and then, assuring me of His presence and constant protection. Even when I'm surrounded by circumstances that would ordinarily cause fear, He has me sit down at ease and eat and enjoy while He fulfills His role as my Protector.

He assures me that goodness and lovingkindness will be mine as long as I follow

If my Shepherd leads the way and He only leads me in His best plan for me, then I don't need to worry about the future. There's no need for me to feel any stress about finances, health, disappointment, disaster. He knows the plans that He has for me, to give me a future and a hope.[5]

He promises to never leave me

Psalm 23 ends with a wonderful assurance: "I will dwell in the house of the LORD forever." That means I'll never be abandoned, exchanged, sold, or thrown out on my own. My Shepherd and I have a lifetime to live together in stability and security.

LIVING IT OUT—IN SECURITY

The Lord wants us to live securely. And we've seen that He's given us all we need to live that way. So the choice is up to us. In her book *Becoming a Woman of Purpose*, Cynthia Heald writes, "In a sense, I have a choice of living as a secure, beloved child of the King, or living as an anxious, frustrated child whose God is not all-powerful or compassionate."[6]

Have you ever watched an anxious, frustrated woman wring her hands and tremble and worry? You begin to wonder how big her God is, don't you? If God is who He says He is and you truly believe it, you will experience rest from knowing He's at work, peace from knowing He's in control, and security from knowing He'll never leave. You will go through the day with confidence that comes from knowing your Shepherd is leading the way. You will never again have to worry that the One who loves you will leave.

I mentioned earlier that there was a time that I did not live securely. I looked for my security in a mother, a boyfriend, a special friend who would never leave. Only when I discovered that God will never leave me nor desert me was I able to remain stable and secure in the midst of situations that could have made me feel insecure.

You and I face choices every day of whether or not we will live securely, resting in His promises, or live anxiously, doubting our God.

I choose to live securely...in the knowledge of His love that will never leave and His presence that will ever guide. I choose to trust in the staying power of the Shepherd of my heart. *What about you?*

Climbing the Steps to Security

You and I have an opportunity now to begin living securely in the arms of our True Love. But to do that, we must surrender the desire to call the shots, pick the path, and control things ourselves. These suggestions will help you climb the steps to higher ground where you can live securely as a woman much loved:

1. Read Psalm 34 and highlight the ways the Lord responded to and took care of David (answered, delivered, heard, and so on). As you read this psalm, keep in mind that you have a relationship with the same God David did. Now, what portions of this psalm give you security in *your* relationship with the Lord?

2. Think about the things you may have done or continue to do that cause people around you to leave. Then read Romans 8:38-39 slowly, and substitute your name where it says "us" in verse 39. Thank the Lord for the depth of security you have in His love for you.

3. Write your own paraphrase of Psalm 23, relating each instance of the Shepherd's provision to your particular situation. Post this in a place where you will see it often and can turn to it when you begin to entertain thoughts of insecurity. Remember, God's promise to you is not that someone else won't leave you, but that He will never abandon you. Gain peace from the knowledge that though others may forsake you, He will always be there.

4
Understanding How He Sees Me

Celeste was a woman most people would run from. A hard-core methamphetamine addict in her mid-30s, she was just as rough-edged on the inside as she was on the outside. Her looks said "rebel" from her short, spiked hair to her tanned, leathery skin to the bandana she wore tied around her left leg. One day Celeste came by my church for food, a little embarrassed to admit she needed anything. But my husband, the church's pastor, felt compelled to help her. He saw a needy woman who was trapped in a hard exterior. He prayed with her before she left with her bag of food.

Two weeks later, Celeste found herself in a jail cell. Arrested for burglary, she had hit rock bottom. Alone, with nothing but time on her hands, she began to think about her life and where it was going. She remembered a prayer offered on her behalf two weeks earlier. And in that jail cell, this hardened woman knelt and accepted Christ as Savior and Lord of her life.

Celeste showed up at church the first Sunday she was out of jail. My husband introduced me to her, but I couldn't believe she was the same woman I saw a month earlier when she came by the church to ask for help. Her hopeless eyes now shone with brightness and her face glowed with a radiance that I hadn't seen in a long time. Her glow came from a new knowledge of who loved her and it literally changed her entire appearance. I stood there amazed at the beauty of this woman.

When the Spirit of God enters our life He changes us from the inside out. Every woman who has a relationship with Christ has the potential to glow as Celeste does. We just need to remember who loves us and who lives within us. For Celeste, the changing power of Christ—taking her from a life of drugs and hopelessness to a life of hope in Him—causes her to smile and literally bubble with joy.

For some of us, perhaps that work of Christ has become commonplace. Maybe we've known God for so long that we don't remember who we were without Him, so we aren't charged every time we think about the changes He's worked in our lives. Or maybe we're so busy that we've gotten to the point where other things have crowded out God and His relevance in our lives. Maybe we've lost the "magic" of the relationship. We've grown lukewarm in what we've come to expect of God and we put our relationship with Him into cruise-control. We go through life knowing He's there but thinking that He doesn't really make that much of a difference anymore. Our passion has cooled. Our interests have waned. And the One who once caused our hearts to beat faster now barely rouses us at all.

If that's the case, we're overdue for a "new face." We need to get back that brightness in our eyes and that smile that never ceases and reclaim the beauty of the bride of Christ. When we portray a "new face"—one that reflects a heart transformed by the power of God—we, like Celeste, can bubble with joy and know from the depths of our hearts that we are pleasing in the sight of God.

QUEST FOR BEAUTY

Every woman wants to be beautiful. Perhaps there's something within us that longs to express and reflect the beauty God created in us. I think part of the reason we want to look beautiful is to be desirable, to be sought-after. When we believe we look great, we feel great and we believe we are worth something and wanted by someone.

I want my husband to always find me desirable. As I get older, I want him to still think I'm beautiful. It makes me feel good to know that he is pleased with how I look. So I stand in front of the mirror every morning, making sure I am presentable to him in a pleasing way.

I know a woman (I'll call her Jill) who wants her husband to find her desirable, too. Unfortunately, she is never quite certain if her husband is happy with her. So she continues to change her hair color and make-up and experiment with new diets and fashions to get the desired response from her husband. "When he says to me, 'Babe, you're beautiful,' then I'll know this is what he likes," she once told me.

By the time Jill starved herself gauntly thin, bleached her hair to a ghostly white, and used up her 50 bonus hours in the solar tanning bed, she began to think that perhaps the thin, blond, and tanned look was too boring for her husband. So she began considering a daring change—to red hair, lots of make-up, and a bit more meat on her bones. Jill hoped to win her husband's love by changing her appearance and making herself more "desirable." Unfortunately, she was attempting to be someone she wasn't in order to hear her husband say "Babe, you're beautiful."

In our relationship with Christ, we never have to live as Jill does. We've seen in the previous chapter the security we have in our relationship with God and the fact that He will never leave us or forsake us—regardless of how we look on the outside or inside. We've also learned that He accepts us for who we are in spite of our physical imperfections, the mistakes of our past, and our sins. With the knowledge that we are accepted and we will always be His, we then come to the issue of how to be pleasing in His sight. The great news is that His heart is fully committed to us. We don't have to do a thing to ourselves to make Him love us more.

PLEASING OUR HEAVENLY HUSBAND

As brides of the Lord Jesus Christ, however, we as women want our Heavenly Husband to be pleased with us, just as we would try to please our husbands or a man we are hoping to impress. To please Him, then, we need to know what it is He desires of us and how we can best meet His expectations. Unlike Jill, we know exactly what it is that our "Husband" expects of us and what will draw His heart even closer to ours.

We learned in chapter two that when we are covered in the righteousness of Christ through salvation, we are acceptable and presentable in God's sight. In fact, God's Word calls us "new creatures"—spotless and perfect in regards to our sin.[1] There's absolutely nothing we can do to make God love and accept us more than He already does. But there *are* several things we can do to please Him and be not just acceptable, but *beautiful* in His sight.

LOOKING IN THE MIRROR

Physical beauty, for most of us, is a result of extra effort in front of the mirror. And spiritual beauty is no different. But I'm not talking about your bathroom mirror, of course. I'm talking about spending time in front of *God's* mirror—the Word of God. James 1:23 says a person who reads the Bible and doesn't apply it to her life is like someone who looks in a mirror and then forgets what she saw. Only when a person repeatedly looks into a mirror and makes an effort to remember the image will she know what she looks like. Likewise, only when we read the Scriptures all the time will we know what our hearts look like before the living God and will we be able to let His Spirit wash us clean and make us presentable and pleasing in God's sight.

By looking in God's Word every morning and letting Him fix us up, we will be able to face the day—and face our Lord—with a "new face." Now, if you're like many women today, you're probably thinking that you just don't have time to read the Bible every day. Besides, you go to church to learn what the Bible says. And you read it every now and then before you go to sleep at night. But that's about all your busy schedule can afford. Well, let me ask you this: Would you consider getting up in the morning and going through your day—and meeting other people—without ever looking in the mirror? *Well, someone told me on Sunday what I looked like, and I did manage a few peeks at myself this week before going to bed. That's going to have to be enough. I really don't have any more time.* None of us would give that response, would we? After all, a smudge of dirt could be on our face and if someone wasn't kind and caring enough to point it out, we'd go through the day—and possibly the next day—looking smudged and unpresentable.

It's the same with our hearts as it is with our faces. If we truly want our Heavenly Husband to see us as beautiful, we need to go to His mirror and let Him show us what our heart looks like *every morning* before going through our day. When His Word shows us what we look like and calls to our mind unconfessed sin, attitudes that must be adjusted, or priorities that need to be realigned, we can let Him do the needed "makeover." But if we look in our spiritual mirror only at bedtime, the world out there is going to see our worn-out face rather than our renewed face.

It's amazing how God's Word works like a mirror. Hebrews 4:12 says the Word of God is "living and active and sharper than any two-edged sword, and piercing as far as the division of soul and spirit, of both joints and marrow, and able to judge the thoughts and intentions of the heart." Wow! That sounds more like a microscope or one of those lighted magnifier mirrors that shows every pore on your skin! But our hearts and minds need that kind of microscope—especially if we want every part of us to be pure and pleasing in His sight.

God's mirror does a great job of *exposing* to us what we cannot see, *deep-cleaning* for us what we cannot reach, and *fixing* for us what we can't begin to repair. And as God's Word shows us the work that needs to be done on our hearts, we can rest easy with this truth: God will never ask us to a) clean up our past; b) do something we're not capable of doing; or c) become someone other than who He created us to be.

RAHAB'S MAKEOVER

God did quite a makeover years ago on a woman named Rahab. She was a prostitute. Probably many men felt she was beautiful, or at least told her so. But the Lord knew what was really going on inside. She was a sinner. A woman living in rebellion to God. A woman unacceptable in God's sight. But one day, two Israelite spies came to her city to check it out. Their plan was to overtake the city, and if she turned them in to the community leaders she probably would have gotten quite a reward. But Rahab had heard of the God these men served and she was fearful of Him and perhaps even afraid of dying in the emptiness of the life she'd come to know. Rahab had heard of how God had rescued His people, the Israelites, from bondage in Egypt, how He had led them through the Red Sea on dry land, and how He had cleared out nations that opposed Israel. Something within her longed to be a part of this people who had a God who protected them and loved them.

So Rahab hid the spies on her roof and lied to her government about their whereabouts. She did this on the condition that the two men would promise to spare her and her family from the pending destruction. She knew this was her only hope of redemption from her past. The men did remember her, and they rescued her. But it was God who had accepted her into the tribe of Israel. God didn't demand that Rahab be treated as a slave among the Israelites because of her shameful past. He didn't try to change her into someone she wasn't. He didn't even make her change her name or her nationality. He took her, accepted her, and made her beautiful in His sight. Considering Rahab's past, she could have been despised and rejected by the Israelites. In fact, prostitution was a sin punishable by death. But we read in Scripture that Rahab married an Israelite. And not just any Israelite, she married a man named Salmon, who was the great-great-grandfather of King David, an ancestor of the long-awaited Messiah, Jesus Christ. There's no doubt about what took place in Rahab's heart when she committed herself to following the will of God. The Lord transformed her from the inside out and she became a beautiful and influential woman among the people of Israel. Because she desired to do God's will, Rahab is remembered not as a prostitute, a traitor to her country or a liar, but a heroine in Israel's history. And she has the prestige of being recorded in the book of Hebrews as a woman of faith.

At first when Rahab wanted to be desired and sought after, she sold her body to the world. But when she found that the world couldn't provide the fulfillment she was seeking, she sold her soul to God, and found that in His love she finally had what she had been seeking. Her body—and the world's use of it—was not what made her beautiful. It was her heart—and God's work in it. And she lived out the rest of her days with a new heart, a new hope, and a new "history" in the eyes of the people.

TAKING THE BEAUTY QUOTIENT

Rahab's example shows how God can take even the most unlikely of people and transform them into vessels of honor for His glory. But what about you and me? For most of us, the change God wants to bring about in our lives won't be as drastic as going from a prostitute to a pillar of faith. But we may need some other kind of "facelift." You may be a middle-aged mother whose face shows signs of being worn out and tired of giving. You may be quite young, but feel old from guilt or some sort of baggage in your life. You may be an older woman who feels you're no longer needed. Or you may simply be an ordinary Christian woman who has lost that loving feeling with the Lord and you want to get back that sparkle in your eyes. Regardless of your situation in life, God can do anything with anyone who is willing to stand before His mirror and take His advice.

What exists in *your* life that keeps you from going before God's mirror and being beautiful in His sight? A feeling that you're doing fine fixing yourself up on your own? A focus on external rather than internal beauty? An attitude displeasing to God that you're refusing to confront? For many of us, it's simply a busyness that claims there's no time. If so, then we need to a make a change of priorities and start a new daily routine.

STARTING A BEAUTY REGIME

God's Word tells us several things we can do on a daily basis to maintain our beauty in God's sight and to make ourselves pleasing to Him:

Rise early and present yourself before Him

David, whom Scripture calls a man after God's heart, knew well the habit of rising early in the morning and pouring his heart out to God. "In the morning, O LORD, Thou wilt hear my voice," David prayed in Psalm 5:3. "In the morning I will order my prayer to Thee and eagerly watch." When we truly desire to give God our best every morning, the old defensive phrase, "I'm not a morning person" will melt into the heart response, "I can't wait to meet Him in the morning." Rising early and talking with your God is the next best thing to waking in His arms.

Request a heart that is pure before Him

In David's heartfelt cry for forgiveness, He prayed, "Create in me a clean heart, O God, and renew a steadfast spirit within me" (Psalm 51:10). We have to continually ask God to examine us and then take care of those things that need to be dealt with. Sometimes we are unaware of a heart that is offensive to God, so we must ask Him to show us what He sees. When He reveals His answer to us—either through His Word, through the counsel of others, or through the conviction of the Holy Spirit—it often pierces our hearts and leads us to repentance. By asking God for a new heart each day, we avoid the pitfall of unconfessed sin and take the right step toward being beautiful in His sight.

Rely on the Spirit of God to do the work that you cannot

Cultivating a heart that loves and obeys God is not something that comes naturally. Therefore, we must depend on the Only One who can do that work in us. Relying on our own ability to please God has never pleased Him. Only faith in the Spirit of God that works within us will please God and produce results in our life.[2]

Redirect your focus to the kind of woman God wants you to be

The Bible tells us to not just be concerned about our external appearance—like our hairstyle, jewelry, and clothing—but to concentrate on our inner heart and qualities that won't go out of style, like a gentle and quiet spirit.[3] The Bible says this kind of spirit is precious in the sight of God. It is something He sees as beautiful. When we truly focus on how *God* wants us to look internally and not just on how we want to look externally, we begin to display a "new face" transformed by the power of God.

A VISION OF BEAUTY

I will never forget a particularly vivid encounter with spiritual beauty. I was on the executive committee for a women's conference and I'd been hearing for months about a worship leader named Betsy who would bless us with her presence during our three-day conference. "Betsy will just transform that place with her worship," the director told me with a gaze in her eyes. "You will be blessed when you worship with Betsy," another woman confirmed. "Betsy is awesome." The praise and admiration went on and on.

Who is this spiritual superwoman named Betsy? I wondered. I imagined a tall woman with a powerful set of lungs and a dynamic personality. But months later, when this Betsy walked into our hotel room to pray with us the night before the conference began, she wasn't anything like I imagined. She was tiny—about five feet tall at the most. She didn't look any older than a teenager. She had very short hair and large teeth. *Hmmm,* I thought to myself. *This Betsy isn't at all what I pictured. She must have some outstanding voice.*

The next morning, when she took the stage with her guitar (which was as big as she was), and opened her Bible to read a passage, she was transformed into a vision of beauty before my eyes. She had such an aura about her and such a radiance—it was as if she glowed from being in God's presence. When she opened her mouth to sing, I was so captivated by her joy and her expression of worship that I don't even remember what her voice sounded like (except that she said the name "God" in a very different and distinct way, as if she'd experienced Him in a way no one else in the room had). As Betsy led us in songs of worship and praise, I marveled at how I no longer saw big teeth, but a beautiful smile. I no longer saw her as short, but as a tall pillar of praise. Betsy no longer looked like a teenager, but rather a mature and beautiful woman with a gift for motivating people to praise and worship God. I literally couldn't take my eyes off of her. I was looking into a face of beauty because I was seeing a heart that reflected the image of God.

On the last day of the conference, I told Betsy that while she was on stage, I felt as if I were watching Jesus. Something about her smile and her eyes and her heart of worship made me see beyond her and catch a glimpse of the Most High. Betsy responded by saying, "Praise God. Each time I get up on stage I pray that people will see Him instead of me." Betsy had become so Christlike in her own life that it powerfully motivated me in my own effort to look like Christ.

Perhaps you know a woman whose heart is so in tune with God that she radiates a presence that you, too, want to reflect. Chances are, that woman is familiar with rising early to present herself to God, requesting a pure heart, relying on the Spirit, and asking God to direct her focus all the day long.

COUNTING THE BEAUTY BENEFITS

When you begin to follow these four steps to spiritual beauty, you will find your "new face." It may be one that bubbles over with joy like Celeste's. Or it may be one that radiates the presence of God like Betsy's. You may begin to notice less "worry lines" around your eyes because of a new peace you have found by trusting in the promises of God's Word. You may find you have less "blemishes" of bitterness, gossip, and a self-centered attitude that may have marred your appearance. You may notice a gentle and quiet spirit that begins to transform your character and leave you a quiet, mysterious beauty to your husband or friends. Others may begin to notice your smile as you become more of an optimistic person and the cancer of cynicism fades from your face. And your eyes may begin to glow with a love and compassion that wasn't there before.

You can be assured of this: When your heart is in place, it will show on your face. You will be amazed at the power of God's Word to completely transform your heart and make you more Christlike in appearance.

PUTTING IT ALL TOGETHER

So what do you think? Are you ready to ditch your old routine and begin a new one that promises to leave you looking better than before? Do you want to glow again with the knowledge that your heart is right and you're beautiful in God's sight? Then start today. You have nothing to lose but the old you.

When you begin to maintain a daily routine of being washed by His Word and perfected by His likeness, you can be confident that you are pure and pleasing in His sight. And knowing you are pleasing and beautiful to our Heavenly Husband will do wonders for your earthly love life as well. There is nothing more attractive and appealing than a woman whose heart is right with God. Like Celeste—and Betsy—it shines in her eyes, shows in her smile, and flows through her actions. Knowing how God sees you truly *can* change your life—and your looks.

Looking in the Spiritual Mirror

❧

Are you ready for the new you, spiritually? Okay, then, let's go. The biggest step is just doing it. Here are some suggestions for your time in front of "God's mirror" so you can grow in your internal beauty. Remember, start with the heart, and your face will fall into place.

1. Think about what you do to make yourself physically beautiful every day. Now spend some time thinking about what you need to do for your spiritual beauty. What actions or attitudes are keeping you from being the most attractive you can be for your Heavenly Husband?

2. Set a date, time, and place for meeting with the Lord every day to go over your "spiritual beauty routine." To help you be consistent, put a note on your refrigerator that says "No Bible, No Breakfast." Or, tape a note to your mirror that says "God's Mirror First." It's amazing what conviction in this area will do for your discipline...and your spiritual appearance!

3. Write out your inner-beauty goals for the Lord in the form of a prayer to Him. Place it in your Bible where you'll see it every time you look into God's mirror.

4. Ask a trusted Christian woman to hold you accountable for maintaining your inner beauty. Remember, unlike your physical face, which is worked on from the outside for external benefits, the spiritual "face" is worked on from the inside for eternal benefits. No one should really know what you're doing to cultivate your inner face except the Lord (and your accountability person).

5. As a personal project, take some time to study the words *pure, clean, holy,* and *beautiful* (or *beauty*) and how they are used in Scripture. Begin by looking up the words in your Bible's concordance and reading every verse you can find that contains these words. Write down all you learn about them. Keep a running list or journal of instructions on how you can be pure, clean, right, holy, and beautiful before the Lord.

Part II

Growing Together

You've made it through the first step of getting
started in your relationship with the Lord.
Hopefully by now you are gaining confidence
that He truly is the Only One who satisfies, and
that He accepts you, He will never leave you, and
He sees you as beautiful in His eyes.
Now it's time to enter into the next phase of the
relationship: growing together. In these next five
chapters, we'll discover how to approach Him,
how to be His "best friend," how to delight Him,
how to avoid disappointing Him and how to
hear His loving voice. By learning what He's
like, what He expects of you and how to
interact with Him, you'll be on your way to
cultivating greater intimacy with the
Lover of your soul.
Stay with me, my friend. As you get
to know these very personal
aspects of your One True
Love, you'll be ready to
go the distance with
Him.

5
Approaching Him with Confidence

We all know people who are difficult to approach. For some of us, it's our boss and we just can't get up the nerve to ask for a raise. Sometimes it's our husband, and we aren't sure how to tell him that we overdrew the checking account again. Sometimes it's a friend who responds and reacts to things differently than we do. Regardless of the type of relationship, if the other person isn't approachable, we have a difficult time establishing trust and intimacy.

I learned the hard way that approaching someone who isn't ready to receive me could cost a friendship.

APPROACHING THE UNAPPROACHABLE

Shirley and I met through a Bible study at church. She would call me now and then for comfort or advice when she was having difficulty in her marriage. Though we were from two separate worlds and had little in common, she took a liking to me and eventually asked me to disciple her in her Christian walk. Shirley and I spent several months studying the Word together, applying it to our lives, sharing the concerns of our hearts, and praying with one another. Naturally, through that process, we became close friends—or, at least I thought we had. Although she shared her innermost thoughts with me and I kept those things in confidence, I still felt there was something missing between us. Somehow I sensed that I couldn't really bare my soul to *her*. I realized after a while that the one thing that hindered our relationship from going deeper was the feeling that I couldn't approach her with what was on my mind. If Shirley was having a bad day, anything I said to her could evoke a biting response. If I questioned her about an action or her motives, she would hang up the phone on me or walk away. If I said something that she didn't quite understand, she would blurt out a rude response. While she could be extremely patient and generous toward me at times, there were other times when she became quite nasty. I just never knew what to expect. For the most part I walked on eggshells around her, doing whatever I could to avoid conflict or confrontation so I wouldn't provoke her wrath.

A year and a half into our friendship, I realized it was time to confront Shirley about this problem because it was beginning to be destructive among the women in our church. Other women were noticing her "unapproachable" ways and were keeping themselves at a safe distance. Some interpreted her looks or actions as a warning to stay away. She was offending others without realizing it. And I, being the woman she had asked to disciple her, took it upon myself to talk to her about her attitude.

After praying and seeking direction from Scripture, I gently pulled Shirley aside one Sunday morning after church. But after a few words into my conversation with her, I realized by the look in her eyes that I must have picked the "wrong day" to do this. I put my hand on her shoulder to convey to her that my words were not a vicious attack, but a concern I was trying to express in a loving way. She responded by physically pushing me out of her presence. After a long phone conversation the following afternoon, Shirley decided she no longer wanted anything to do with me. She never spoke to me again.

WHO CAUSES YOU TO TIPTOE?

My husband can tend to be unapproachable if he's not in a good mood. He isn't bitter or pushy as Shirley had become, but he is not one to talk or receive things well if he's hungry, under stress, or angry about a situation. To be on the safe side, I usually think through a few questions before approaching him: *What kind of day did he have? Who is the last person who spoke with him and what was said? Is he feeling okay physically? Is he hungry, tired, stressed-out?* Once I gather enough data, I decide if I should take the chance and attempt to talk.

Maybe you know someone who is unapproachable or just keeps you guessing as to when you should come around. It's emotionally exhausting to have to wonder about when you can speak your mind, share your heart, or offer a suggestion. But it's a relief to know that with our Heavenly Husband we never have to worry. God is always 100-percent approachable. No guessing—no risks, just do it.

WE CAN BE CONFIDENT

The Bible tells us the Lord is a compassionate God[1] who understands what we bring to Him because He, too, through the person of Jesus Christ, has faced the things we face.[2] Thus we are told to "draw near with confidence to the throne of grace, that we may receive mercy and may find grace to help in time of need" (Hebrews 4:16). We can draw near to God with confidence! Now let's think about that concept a bit. He is the God of the universe. He has billions of people and situations to deal with. Consequently it's easy for me to assume He's too busy to care about me. Yet He tells me to approach Him with confidence—*anytime* with *anything*. Now that's incredible!

The Bible tells me that God counts the number of hairs on my head (Matthew 10:30), collects each of my tears in a bottle, and records in a book every place that I wander (Psalm 56:8). That pretty much sounds like I'm the object of His affection and someone He wants dearly to commune with. If I'm that precious to Him, wouldn't He want to hear what's on my mind?

Of course He would. And the same is true for you, too. His Word says to "pour out your heart before Him" because He is a refuge for us (Psalm 62:8). That means we can get things off our mind, blow steam, and vent our feelings to Him, and it's safe. We don't need to worry about the aftermath, any subjective feelings, or a silent response. God won't play the "get even" game or nod His head like He heard and go on reading the paper. Like one enthralled with the object of his affection, He eagerly awaits our approach.

WHAT HOLDS YOU BACK?

Okay, so God is approachable. But why do we still hesitate to approach Him? Is it because we feel that what we want to say is of little importance or consequence to Him? Is it because we feel we've gone to Him with our quota for the day? Is it because there is sin in our life and we aren't sure He will listen? Or is it because it's been so long since we last talked to Him that we wouldn't really know where to start?

No matter what the issue, you can bring it to God. Just so you can see how true that is, let's suppose for a moment what would happen if God were moody or impatient with certain people or the circumstances around Him. The accounts we have of Him would read differently, wouldn't they? For example, when Hannah made a vow to the Lord, pleading with Him to give her a child, the Lord could have responded, "Hannah, quit your sniveling. I hear *every single year* about how much Elkanah's other wife mistreats you and how unfulfilled and unhappy you are because you don't have a child. Get over it! And get a life!" But Hannah's loving God didn't say that. He listened to her vow and He graciously granted her request for a child.[3]

If the Lord wanted to teach us a lesson every time we came to Him with a complaint or question, He would've put Martha of Bethany in her place when she blamed Him for the death of her brother. "Lord, if You had been here, my brother would not have died," Martha said accusingly to the Son of God after He refused to come back with her and heal Lazarus when he was still sick.[4] But rather than be annoyed at her accusation and lecture her for always having to have someone to blame, Jesus offered Martha some encouraging words: "Your brother shall rise again." A few minutes later, Martha's sister, Mary, saw Jesus and spoke the same exact words as her sister: "Lord, if You had been here, my brother would not have died." Again, rather than throw up His hands at the sisters' complaining and whining, Jesus related to their pain and *was deeply moved in spirit.*[5]

And when Peter saw Jesus on the shore after His resurrection, and jumped out of his boat and swam to Him, Jesus, you'd think, would have turned up his nose and said, "I'm outta here, Peter. Just three days ago you denied even knowing Me and now you want to be My best friend? Forget it. Get your own breakfast. This here's for James and John. They know a little something about how to be a *real* friend." But Jesus didn't do that. Although Peter had denied Jesus, the Lord still cooked Peter's breakfast! Then He sat down and comforted and encouraged Peter with words He knew the disciple would ponder and treasure the rest of his life. In a very tender manner, Jesus assured His most clumsy and boisterous disciple that, although he had denied Jesus in the face of adversity, he would one day die for Him out of loyalty. Jesus knew it, and He wanted Peter to know that He knew it. It was as if Jesus was saying, "I forgive you. I know your heart, and I know you're going to do great things for Me."[6]

If God were unapproachable, He would have given up on me long ago over the countless times I have come to Him with doubts about how He's going to provide for me and questions about how I'm supposed to serve His people. God has shown me time and again that He will provide all I need. He has shown me many times through His Word that I am called to be obedient to Him, not to be responsible for how His people respond. Yet I still question and complain. I still doubt and fret. And God, in His loving kindness, patiently listens and answers and continues to provide.

What Does He Want?

While God longs for us to approach Him, it's vital that we know *how* to approach Him.

There are several things to keep in mind when approaching God—whether it be to confess our sins, to intercede for another, or to simply enter His presence and feel His love.

Approach Him openly

First, we are to approach Him *as we are* with no pretenses. To approach God with no pretenses means I come to Him as I am, with no intention of making Him think I am anything other than who I am. God knows me from the inside out. There's no way I can try to impress Him with big words or pretend to feel a certain way; He's going to see right through it.

Approach Him contritely

Second, we are to approach Him with a spirit that is *sorry for any sin we've committed.* That means no defenses. Approaching God with no defenses means being willing to admit I am wrong. Excusing and rationalizing my sin before God is not His desire for my prayer time with Him. He loves a broken and contrite heart (Psalm 51:17) as opposed to a haughty and proud heart.

Approach Him submissively

Third, we are to approach Him with a heart that is *willing to accept what He wants for us.* That implies no agendas. Approaching God without an agenda means I come to Him without expectations of what I think He should do. I am not to use prayer to convince Him of my will, but to surrender to His. O. Hallesby, in his book, *Prayer,* says, "We make use of prayer to convince God that we see the matter in the right light, that the answer should be given immediately, and should be as we have planned it....We are afraid that God will not permit Himself to be convinced by our prayer, but will do as He wills regardless of our supplications...."[7] When we begin to trust that His will is far better than ours, we will approach with only the expectation that He will take care of us according to His lovingkindness and sovereign plan for us.

Approach Him reverently

Ecclesiastes 5:2 instructs us to "not be hasty in word or impulsive in thought to bring up a matter in the presence of God. For God is in heaven and you are on the earth; therefore let your words be few." Although God wants us to pour out our hearts to Him, He also wants us to remember whom we are addressing. He may be our Lover and our Friend, but He is still our God. Thus, we must approach Him with respect.

Approach Him confidently

As Hebrews 4:16 says, we can approach the Lord confidently because we are clothed in the righteousness of Christ. And when we ask for anything in Christ's name, in accordance with God's will, He hears us (1 John 5:14-15). Just as we would go to the hardware store and ask for something for our husband, who has an established account and excellent credit, we can go to the throne of God and ask for things in the name of our Heavenly Husband, Jesus. He has an established account and excellent credit. He has the Father's ear. Now that is confidence!

Approach Him in faith

Without faith it is impossible to please God, Hebrews 11:6 tells us. And James tells us we must ask in faith if we expect our requests to be taken seriously.[8] Our Heavenly Husband wants to see that we really believe in Him and that we believe He will respond when we ask something of Him.

My earthly husband says that he is disappointed when I ask someone else to do something for me that he can do himself. If I ask our neighbor to move a heavy item for me while Hugh is at work, or to fix something in my house because I feel that my husband is too busy to bother with it, Hugh feels the blow. As my husband, he *wants* to accomplish things for me. And if I ask him for something but ask in a way that implies to him that I really don't think he'll consider my request or take the time to give me what I ask, it takes the wind out of his sails. He wants to be needed by his wife. He wants me to believe in him. It's part of what makes him feel good as a man and a husband. I imagine that part of God's joy in hearing our needs and requests is seeing His bride's hope and dependency on Him. God wants us to ask *Him*, and to ask believing that He will come through.

When we approach God with these things in mind, we can enjoy the bliss of being in His presence and letting Him minister to us. "When the Spirit has taught us that God...Himself decides when and how our prayers are to be answered, then we shall experience rest and peace when we pray."[9]

THE BENEFITS OF APPROACHING HIM

Learning to approach our Heavenly Husband will help us become women who are:

> • **Confident of the power within us to accomplish His will through prayer (1 John 5:14-15).** When we know He hears us, we know we have what we've requested, according to the wisdom and goodness of God. We can be confident as ambassadors for the Lord in that we can accomplish His work through prayer. That's a confidence-building step for any woman!

> • **Capable of doing all things—no matter how difficult—through His strength (Philippians 4:13).** When we realize the pressure is not on us, but on Him who works through us, to accomplish all things, it makes us not only confident, but capable and unstoppable. You are no longer a weak woman when you have the Lord's ear. You are able to do all things through Him who strengthens you!

> • **Consumed with joy from being in His presence (Psalm 16:11).** Being in the presence of God changes people. And it can change you and me as we discover the joy of coming to Him anywhere and anytime to speak what's on our mind.

GO FOR IT!

Now that you've discovered just how approachable

the Lord is, don't you want to rush into His arms and tell Him everything that's on your mind? You will never exhaust His ear. You will never wear Him out. And you will always be blessed just by being in His presence.

Forget those times that your pride has been squashed or your feelings hurt or your dreams dashed because you approached someone who didn't have the time to help, or the heart to hear. You know now that will never happen with the One who lives to love you. So go ahead—run to Him and pour out your heart. You'll find that true love, joy, and peace await you in His arms.

Gaining Confidence in the Throne Room

You can be a confident, capable woman in coming before the throne of God when you keep in mind just how approachable He is. Try working through these steps to gain confidence in approaching *your* True Love.

1. Think of some things you've always wanted to approach God about but never did. Write them out and then tell Him about them. It's easier than you think.

2. Is there something you need to approach your husband or someone else about, but you've always feared doing so? Tell the Lord about it first, and ask Him for the ability to approach the subject in the right way at the right time. Rely on His strength for the confidence you need.

3. Is there anything God may have tried approaching *you* about that you've been a little hesitant to hear? Ask Him now. And tell Him you're willing to receive it from Him and His Word with the same patience and grace He showed you when you came to Him.

6
Making Him My Best Friend

Julie grew up not knowing what it was like to have a friend. She was 18 months old when her father, a pilot in Vietnam, was declared missing in action. Julie's mother, pregnant at the time, took out her anger, bitterness, and resentment over her husband's death on little Julie. For years Julie endured emotional, verbal, and physical abuse from her mother, who was either irate or indifferent toward her daughter.

Longing to feel valued by someone—by anyone—Julie became a habitual liar, trying to please her mother and others by making her stories "better" or making up situations that might create a more favorable atmosphere. But she was ashamed of her lying and, without any self-esteem whatsoever, Julie became extremely withdrawn, very sensitive, and frightened of becoming close to anyone. Because she had grown so weary of being hurt at home, she avoided friendships or relationships so she wouldn't be hurt anywhere else.

Although Julie lived the first half of her life alone—not trusting anyone, not knowing what it was like to have a true friend—she had a vague concept of someone named

Jesus who reportedly loved her and to whom she prayed at night, asking for the strength to stop lying and for the ability to make friends.

By the time Julie reached high school, she figured the love she was seeking might be found in a boyfriend, so she went through several in a few years, not giving anything of herself emotionally, but trying to get so much in return. In her constant search for someone to value her, she kept coming up empty.

During Julie's senior year of high school she began to spend more and more time with Mike, a boy from school who didn't run with the rough crowd like the other kids their age. She had known Mike for six years, but never considered him anything more than a friend—or at least what she knew of a friend. Just about the time Julie was hoping that Mike would ask her out, he called and did so. On their first date, they just talked as friends and watched a movie together, but Julie remembers feeling the warmth of a person who genuinely cared about her. She remembers realizing, for the first time, that someone really valued her as a person. And that night, Julie fell in love with Mike and all he represented to her—care, concern, sincerity, friendship, and unconditional love.

"I finally found someone who loved me—no matter what," Julie recalls about what became a long-term dating relationship with Mike. They dated for five years, while they finished college, and then Julie—the one who never imagined being loved by anyone—married Mike, who had become her best friend.

Mike was the first person in Julie's life to love her unconditionally. And through their dating and married years together, he has been protective, forgiving, even-tempered, patient, and longsuffering. He is truly understanding of who she is. And it was Mike who eventually made Julie realize what a friend she has in Jesus.

"By sending me a friend to love me unconditionally,

God was opening my eyes to the love He has for me," Julie recalled recently with tears in her eyes. "I know Mike's love for me is only one one-millionth of the love God has for me, and that is incomprehensible."

Julie is now 11 years into her marriage with Mike, and 22 years into their friendship. And she has blossomed into a vibrant, outgoing young woman with several close friends. She has even put the bitterness behind her and cultivated a close relationship with her mother. Julie realizes now that by bringing Mike into her life to love her, God was freeing her up from the pain in her past so she could focus her life on God, the One who loves her more than a mother, more than a husband, more than a friend.

When Julie looks back at her life before Mike, and before a full understanding of God's love for her, she marvels at God's protection and guidance and friendship toward her during the times she thought she was alone. As a friend, the Lord protected her, led her on the straight and narrow, and helped her make the right choices. Today Julie calls her life wonderful because she clearly sees the grace of God in her life and because she knows what a friend she has in Jesus.

———

Joani's childhood was the opposite of Julie's. She enjoyed a close relationship with her mother and remembers the two of them being best friends. Similar to Mike's friendship toward Julie, Joani's mom showed her daughter a glimpse of how God relates to us as a friend.

Joani clearly remembers the day she made a conscious decision to utilize her mom as her friend. She was eight or nine at the time and was keeping something from her mom. She remembers her mother extending herself toward her daughter and saying, "Won't you share with me what you're feeling?"

"I realized then that my own mother had an interest in my life and wanted me to share my life with her," Joani said. She told her mother what was on her mind, and her mother offered some wisdom and advice. That was the beginning of a closeness and a communication that would last through the years. Since that morning, Joani has never been afraid to be totally open and honest with her mother because she knows she will receive complete understanding rather than condemnation.

Joani learned, through her friendship with her mother, what a friend she has in Jesus. Like Joani's mom, God sought Joani out as well. He wanted Joani to share with Him every detail of her life and He wanted to share with her His wisdom. But she had to make a conscious decision to involve herself with the Lord, to utilize Him as a friend.

Today Joani lives several hundred miles away from her mother, but the two keep their relationship close by phoning each other often and visiting a few times a year. Just as Joani continues to keep in contact with her mother, she realizes the necessity of constant companionship and communication with the Lord, her best friend. For as long as I've known her, Joani's life has emanated a joy, sincerity, and depth that comes from walking with the One who sticks closer than a mother, closer than a best friend. Joani truly knows what a friend she has in Jesus.

As you've been getting to know the relational side of God, you're probably realizing that He can be a great friend to *you* as well. After all, you've seen that He loves you unconditionally, He accepts you just as you are, He will never leave You, He sees you as perfect—through His Son, Jesus—and He is easy to approach. But have you ever considered Him your best friend? And have you ever considered the Lord thinking of you as *His* best friend?

No matter where you are in life when it comes to friendships—whether you have friends on every corner as Joani does, or you are hesitant to get close to someone (as Julie was)—Jesus is One who sticks closer than a brother, closer than a best friend.

THE TIES THAT BIND

Friendship with Jesus is a concept that can best be understood by looking at our friendships here on earth. Both Julie and Joani gained a fuller understanding of the kind of friend God is through the friendships they experienced with others.

No matter what your background, I'm willing to bet that when you think of a best friend you think of a person, or a type of person, who:

> • *loved you unconditionally (like Mike toward Julie);*
> • *extended their heart toward you (like Joani's mom toward her);*
> • *shared with you the joys of your childhood; or*
> • *expressed loyalty to you by "being there" when you most needed someone.*

We already looked at examples of the first two components of friendship: unconditional love and extending one's self toward another. Now let's look at a couple other examples of how we might bond together with a best friend.

Friendships from the past

My image of a best friend was formed during my early childhood. As far back as I can remember, Stacy and I were best friends. We learned to walk together, talk together, bicycle, and skate together. Stacy lived in the house behind me, so she was always a few steps away. And she was exactly one month older than me, so we were always interested in the same things.

Stacy and I did everything together, every day. We made imaginary countries in the dirt behind my play-house and we wore tights on our heads and pretended we had long "ponytails." We played genies in the hallway closets and had our own "school house" and "library." We dressed like each other so we could be "twins" and we shared secrets and experiences no one else would under-stand. We were literally inseparable. And we often heard our parents say, "They're in their own little world when they're together."

Stacy and I eventually drifted apart as we got older and became interested in different things. But my memo-ries of what I shared with her as a young child constantly remind me of what I can experience today with Jesus: being together every day, trying to look and be like Him, sharing all my secrets with Him, shutting out everything else and being in our own little world together. My child-hood friendship with Stacy showed me what it's like to have a friend in Jesus.

Friendships from loyalty

Janice and JoAnne are an example of friends who became close through their willingness to "be there" for one another throughout their lives.

The two met in junior-high school and a couple years later attended a Billy Graham Crusade together, and there accepted Christ as their personal Savior. Their individual decisions to follow Christ and their friendship with one another were two things they would depend on greatly during some very painful years to come.

While the two young women were still teenagers, JoAnne called Janice one day with the sobering news that her father had died. Janice remembers both of them not saying much, just sobbing over the phone together.

While they were in their twenties, JoAnne stayed with Janice for a while to provide companionship during the long, lonely months that Janice missed her fianceé, who was stationed in Vietnam. Some years after that, when Janice's brother took his own life, JoAnne was there on the other end of Janice's phone, offering words of comfort and encouragement that only a best friend could bring.

And when the women were in their mid-forties, and JoAnne had her leg removed because of health problems, Janice hopped on a plane and went to be with her best friend. But that was the last time they could "be there" for each other. A year later, JoAnne passed away during a surgery to have her other leg removed. Janice again flew a couple hundred miles up to JoAnne's home, but this time to minister to the needs of JoAnne's family. She knew JoAnne would've done the same for her.

It's been five years since Janice lost her best friend, and although she hasn't found another woman to fill the void JoAnne left, she has found in Jesus a sense of joy and completeness she didn't think she could feel again. Janice's relationship with JoAnne showed her what a friend she has in Jesus.

WHAT A FRIEND WE HAVE IN JESUS

If all this talk about friendship makes you sad because you've never really had a best friend, you're in for a surprise. Or, if you've been fortunate enough to experience the joy of many fulfilling friendships, you too are in for a surprise. You see, what you have considered a best friend by experience—or always hoped for in a best friend—doesn't even compare to the close companionship you can have with Jesus. Friendship with Him is more fulfilling than a childhood companionship, more bonding than any situation you can experience with a person here on earth, and more intimate than the relationship in which you share all your secrets.

Before I talk about the characteristics of the greatest Friend who ever lived, think for a few moments about your list of qualifications for a best friend.

- *Do you look for loyalty and unconditional love?*
- *Do you want someone with whom you can confide and never have to worry about your secrets being betrayed?*
- *Is it companionship you crave?*
- *Is it quality and quantity time you'd like to have with one special person?*

I know many women who avoid friendships with other women because they've never been able to trust someone long enough to get close to them. These women are tired of being the victim of gossip, being upset by petty arguments, or being burned by betrayal. If you're dealing with some baggage in the friendship department, I want you to stop and consider what you've learned about the Lord already. He *isn't* like anyone else you've met on earth. And when it comes to friendship, He offers something pure and true and unlike anything you've experienced before.

Let me explain just a few of the character qualities of Jesus that I've discovered in my 30-year friendship with Him.

Jesus has always been there

We talked about how we bond with people who have shared our past, shared meaningful experiences with us, or who have "been there" for us. Well, Jesus is One who has always "been there" for me throughout my life.

I was fortunate enough to be introduced to Jesus as a young child. So I remember Him being there—as my best friend—on the first day of kindergarten when I would've otherwise felt lost and alone. I remember Him giving me courage when I started to be afraid after accidentally locking myself in my grandmother's bathroom at the age of seven. I remember His powerful presence by my bed, where I lay for three weeks with scarlet fever at the age of nine. Yes, Jesus and I, as best friends, have gone through a lot together.

My Best Friend was still by my side when I, as a teenager, waited in an out-of-state emergency room to learn of my baby brother Steven's condition after falling from a park slide while we were vacationing. He not only gave me peace during that time of uncertainty, but He took care of my brother's needs, healing his tiny body from a fractured skull and collarbone.

A year later, Jesus was still there to comfort me when I learned of my grandmother's tragic death in a car accident and I helped my mother cope with the loss.

During my adult years, Jesus ministered to me every morning when I was on my knees praying for my brother Dan's safety as a soldier on the front lines of a ground war in the Middle East. When no one else knew what to say to give me strength and faith during that time, God's words (in His Word) were there every morning, every evening, holding me up, keeping me strong and hopeful.

And Jesus stayed with me—when I would have otherwise been alone—for three days in the cancer ward of a children's hospital as I watched my 18-month-old daughter undergo a series of tests to determine if she had cancer or leukemia. He listened to my questions, understood my anxiety, filled me with His peace, embraced me in His arms, and held my hand during the night when I couldn't sleep.

From fearful days as a child to uncertain times as a parent, I've never seen the Lord let me down. He was always there to comfort me when no one else was. He rushed to my side when no one else could. He knew what to say when no one else did. That is a true friend.

Jesus has always kept His promises

It's important to be able to trust a best friend, to take a friend at his or her word. In all the time I've known Jesus, He has never broken any of His promises. In His Word, He has promised to:

- *never leave me (Hebrews 13:5), and He never has.*
- *always love me (Romans 8:38-39), and He still does.*
- *forgive my sins and never bring them up again (Isaiah 43:25). That's just what He did.*
- *direct me on a straight path (Proverbs 3:6). That's what He continues to do.*
- *always provide for me (Philippians 4:13). And He always has.*

Jesus has never let me down

The Lord has always provided for me—financially, physically, emotionally, and spiritually—just like He said He would. He's always made things work out when I've done them according to His way (Romans 8:28). He's always supplied what I've needed when I've sought Him first (Matthew 6:33). And at times when I thought He wasn't being faithful, He led me to His Word in Isaiah 55:11, where He explains His ways are not our ways and we sometimes cannot comprehend why He does what He does, but He still remains faithful. In fact, He continues to be faithful to me even when I am not faithful to Him.[1]

Proverbs 18:24 says, "A man of many friends comes to ruin, but there is a friend who sticks closer than a brother." In my life, I have found that one friend to be Jesus.

During the times in your life when it seemed everyone else had walked out on you, He was still there, wasn't He? Singing songs of comfort, whispering words of encouragement, being a friend to call upon in time of need. Jesus doesn't let His friends down.

Jesus has loved me sacrificially

Jesus Himself said the true test of friendship is whether one will sacrifice himself for another. He wasn't just talking about making little sacrifices here and there, like dropping what you're doing to run over and be with a friend in her time of need. Jesus was talking about sacrificing one's *life*.

"Greater love has no one than this, that one lay down his life for his friends," Jesus told his disciples in John 15:13. Then He added, "*You* are my friends" (verse 14). And He backed up His words a few days later by dying for them. Keep in mind that what Jesus did to prove His love for His friends wasn't just for His disciples; it was for you and me, too. No other friend on this earth could make the kind of sacrifice Jesus made for us when He died a death that *we* deserved, instead of Him. Yet He took our penalty upon Himself willingly, out of love for those He wanted to call His friends.

Jesus has motivated me to keep the friendship going

We all have friends that we, at times, desire more from.

I wish he had a little more time for me...

I just wish we could see each other more...

If we're really that close, why does she just drop off the face of the earth sometimes and never even call me...?

I wish we could talk about that, but it has just never come up...

Jesus has never left me wanting something more from Him as a friend. And He apparently has this effect on everyone who really knows Him and comes to love Him.

Like I said earlier, Jesus had friends while on this earth. The ones we know the most about were his 12 followers or disciples, whom Jesus called friends. These were the friends with whom He ate His meals, explained His teachings, revealed the mysteries of God, and shared what was on His heart. Jesus had such an impact on His circle of friends and created such a loyalty among them that all but one (Judas—who turned out to not be such a good friend, after all) chose to live for Him and ultimately to die for Him. Jesus died for them; they died for Him. Theirs was a friendship and loyalty that even death couldn't dissolve.

Jesus offers that kind of friendship to us as well. The only condition He places upon us, in order for us to call ourselves His friends, is to obey Him.[2]

WHAT ABOUT YOU?

I've told you the kind of friend Jesus has been to me, but what has He done for *you?* I mentioned that Jesus has always been there for me. And He's been there for you, too. How do you know? Because before you were born, He knew your name and what you were going to do with your life (remember chapters 2 and 3?). That means He's been a childhood friend whether or not you've realized it.

Think of the times that you knew "someone" was watching over you. Think of the days when you were lonely, but somehow you got by. Do you remember times that you felt someone was rooting for you but you couldn't quite figure out who?

Perhaps you do remember Jesus being there for you

and actually being your best friend at one time or another. But unfortunately, many of us go through a "Jesus friendship" as a young Christian the same way we go through a "girl friendship" as a young child. Like my friendship with Stacy, we stick with a Jesus friendship as long as it's fun and meets our immediate needs, and then we begin to develop interests that take us in a different direction from our Best Friend. We sometimes get to the point where we rarely even talk with Him anymore. And we find ourselves, at times, fondly remembering the way it used to be. Before we realize it, we've replaced our Best Friend with someone or something else.

REUNITING WITH YOUR BEST FRIEND

Have you replaced the Lord as your Best Friend? If so, who did you replace Him with? A boyfriend? A husband? Your sister? Your mother? A girlfriend with whom you share everything?

Sometimes it's not another person that replaces Jesus in your life; it's just the busyness of life or circumstances that take you in a different direction from Him. Sometimes your priorities change, without you realizing it, and you find you have less time for Him. I'm willing to bet that if you feel distant from Jesus, it wasn't a conscious choice or a sudden event that changed around your priorities. It was probably more of a series of gradual changes, like a career or marriage or move that led you to circles of people who weren't friends with Jesus. Perhaps all of life felt like a predictable routine for you and you slowly lost your motivation to do things with Him everyday. Or, maybe it was the feeling that you needed a best friend who could do more with you, like shop, go out to lunch, watch old movies with you, or talk with you daily on the phone.

As we've already seen our God in heaven can very much fulfill the needs we have here on earth. And a close friendship is one of those needs. If the Lord is not your best friend right now, I want to share with you how He can be. And if you used to be good friends but that memory is fading, I want to lead you back to the comfort of a close companionship with Him.

1. *Accept Him for who His Word says He is, not who you want Him to be*

We learned in chapter 2 that God accepts us for who we are. We must, likewise, accept Him for who He really is, not what we've imagined Him to be. His Word tells us who He is, and sometimes if He does not respond to us in the way we'd like or provide for us in the way we'd prefer or give to us what we wanted to have, we get frustrated or discouraged and believe He isn't a good friend. Remember, His ways are not our ways.[3] And we must realize He is God. Although He calls us His friends, He still keeps an appropriate line of respect. He is also our Master and our Lord.

2. *Acknowledge that He's always been there and you are the one who has drifted*

Remember our talk in chapter 3 about God's footprints that "may not be known" when He is leading us through the waters? A day has not gone by in which your Friend was not there with you. He has always been there because His Word says there's nowhere we can go, even in a rebellious state of mind, where He will not go with us.[4] If we have felt distant from God, it's because we no longer acknowledged His presence or actively included Him in our life. Upon realizing what has happened, we need to invite Him back into our life and reconnect the bonds of friendship.

3. *Adore Him as the One you want to be with and be like*

When I was a child, there were certain girls that I just had to be friends with because I wanted to be like them. They were so popular, so pretty, so all-together. That may seem childish now, but that kind of adoration for God and a feeling that we need to be close to Him is good to have. When we admire Him, want to be with Him, want to be seen with Him, and want to imitate all He does, then we know the meaning of being best friends with God.

4. *Attach yourself to Him like glue*

Did you ever have a friend who always followed you around? She always wanted to be in your presence. No matter who you were with and what you were doing, she was there, wanting to enjoy your companionship. That's the kind of person we need to be in pursuing our friendship with God. But unlike those who get annoyed with that type of attention, God will embrace it. In Jeremiah 29:13, God says we will find Him when we search for Him with all our heart. Like the woman in Jesus' parable who continually pestered the judge until he gave her what she wanted,5 we should persist and persist in cultivating a friendship with the Lord.

5. *Avoid becoming complacent*

It's tragic to know Christ but not to love Him intensely, because then we are lukewarm—not hot for God, but not cold to Him, either.

We can all think of a lukewarm friendship—one that has grown stale, like a friend who never calls or writes. God indicates in Revelation 3:15-16 that He *loathes* a lukewarm relationship and that He would rather have us be cold to Him altogether than to be indifferent. He implies in His Word that He would rather have us never have known Him than to have experienced His friendship and walked away like it didn't matter. A true friend makes a lasting impression. And a true friend is one that we want to hold onto for life. So how can we experience the unconditional love of God and the true depths of friendship with the Lover of our soul and not respond wholeheartedly? As with Julie, God's love should bring us to our knees.

Obviously Jesus had what you needed and wanted for you to come into a relationship (and friendship) with Him. But always make sure you continue to want and need what He has. He won't change in what He offers you. He is unchangeable. It is we who lose interest, believing we can find what we need elsewhere, or becoming interested in things or people other than Him. Guard your heart to make sure He is always your best friend. And if He's not, ask yourself why.

6. *Allow Him into your life by sharing the little things*

It's the day-to-day chats, the little things, the good-morning call, or "How was your day?" conversations that keeps friendships alive and fresh. Keep yours alive with God by keeping the channels of communication open. That means sharing with Him your secrets, your thoughts, the stuff you might think too silly to share with anyone else but a best friend. Laugh about some of the more embarrassing moments in your life and thank Him for being with you in those times. Remind Him of the times you had no idea what He was doing and how surprised and delighted you were to find out how God worked out those situations for the best. Cherish your times together and talk about them often.

7. *Assign Him first place each day*

As a child, I rushed home from school every day to play with Stacy. She was my first priority—I couldn't wait to be with her. Are you rushing to be with the Lord before anything else in your day? (Remember our talk in chapter 4 about rising early to meet Him? It isn't just to look in the "mirror," it's to be with Him and enjoy His fellowship.) Make Him priority No. 1 so nothing else comes between your friendship. Not time. Not busyness. Not another person. With God, we need to prioritize prayer, worship, and spending time in His presence so we can fully enjoy His friendship.

8. *Allow quantity time for Him*

We talk about quality time and it's importance to any relationship. But now people are discovering that quantity time is just as important. I once complained to a boyfriend that he never had enough time for me. He then admitted, "We all make time to do what we really want." That was his way of saying he didn't really want to be with me that much. As much as I despised hearing that quip, I never forgot it. And to this day, I think twice before telling someone I don't have time for this or that. We do make the time for whatever is extremely important to us.

If the Lord is our priority relationship, we will make the time to be with Him. And we will do it frequently. For me, that time is three times a day: mornings at 5:00 a.m. when it's just Him and me looking into His Word; mid-mornings, when the two of us go on a two-mile walk and talk about our relationship; and in the evenings when I lay in bed, He's the last One I talk to as I drift off to sleep. In the case of building a friendship with Jesus, quantity time makes a quality friendship.

9. *Aspire to grow in the friendship*

How far do you want your friendship with God to grow? How close do you really want to be?

I want my relationship with God to be like that of Enoch's. The Bible says Enoch "walked with God" for 300 years![6] What a legacy! We don't have any details of what Enoch *did* during his life, other than that he "walked with God." Enoch and God must have had some great talks as they walked. And they must have been close because God longed for Enoch's friendship so much that He "took him" home rather than leaving him to die a natural death. Enoch and God's friendship was so deep, so personal that it involved walks and talks. I want to share that kind of deep intimate friendship with the Lord, too. Don't you?

START WALKING

So, what do you think? When it comes to friendship and what you'd like in a best friend, does Jesus fit the bill? When you think of who you want to share the best of the best with, is He the One? After all, He has been there throughout your childhood; He even knew you before you were born. He has been through whatever you have, because of the way He never lets you out of His sight. And whether you've noticed His presence or not, He has been right beside you during the good times and the bad, just like a best friend. Even if you've lost touch with Him for a while, you can pick up where you left off, just like we do with our friends in this life.

Begin walking with God and discovering what a friend you have in Jesus. But don't just walk the block. Go the extra mile with Him. Make your friendship with God one that is so close, so fulfilling, that the world looks on with envy.

There's an old hymn that talks of that kind of friendship with God, as the two meet every day in a garden:

And He walks with me, and He talks with me,
And He tells me I am His own,
And the joy we share as we tarry there
None other has ever known. [7]

Be His best friend. And you may even leave behind a legacy that reads, "She *walked* with God."

Becoming His Best Friend

❧

Do you need a few ideas of things you can do to go the extra mile with God and cultivate a closer friendship? Remember, He is waiting to spend more time with you, become closer to you, and be a more intimate friend. But you must take the initiative and invite Him to become more involved in your life. Here's how:

1. Take a walk with the Lord this week. Try to find a quiet place where the two of you won't be interrupted. You could walk in your local park, along the beach, or around your neighborhood. Talk with Him as if He were right there (because He is) and thank Him for being the perfect friend.

2. Think of ten qualities of a "best friend." As you think about how Jesus encompasses each of those qualities, determine in your heart and mind that *you* will be that kind of friend to the Lord Jesus.

3. Define some goals for your friendship with God. Do you want to get beyond the acquaintance stage? Do you want to be "best friends"? Do you want to start being there for Him as He has been there for you? Write your goals in the form of a prayer.

4. Write a letter to your best friend, Jesus. Recount all the things He's done for you in the time you've known

Him. Remind Him of special times you've had together and recommit yourself to Him as a friend who will never leave Him or let Him down. Commit to Him in the letter at least one thing you will do this week to show your love and loyalty to your Best Friend.

7
Clinging to What He Desires

As I sat in my study, trying to concentrate on my writing, the noise in the kitchen grew louder. Water had been running incessantly, pots and pans were clanging around, and silverware was dropping onto the floor. Irritated by all the commotion, I finally yelled to my six-year-old daughter: "What are you getting into *now?*"

"I'm washing your dishes, Mommy," Dana responded excitedly.

I immediately got up from the computer and entered the kitchen to find her—and the kitchen floor—soaking wet! Bubbly dishes were stacked haphazardly on top of each other in the drying tray. Dana stood there with a grin, obviously pleased at her work and her "surprise" for me. My head said, "Get the mop," but my heart (thank You, Lord) said, "Give her a hug," and I loved up her little wet body and told her how much I appreciated her wonderful surprise for me. Dana knew how much I desired help around the house, and she wanted to please me. In her own way, she was showing me that she loved me.

Besides dishwashing, Dana enjoys drawing pictures.

She knows that when she draws the two of us, or anything else, and puts the words, "I love you, Mom" on the picture, that my eyes light up and I smile and make a big deal over it and place the picture on my refrigerator. Dana loves to see my reaction. So my refrigerator is covered and my file is full of pictures she has drawn for me. Dana knows how much I desire to see her expressions of love toward me. So, she continues to give me drawings to show me that she loves me.

Dana also knows that I like white coconut jelly beans. When she and I go to the mall, it's tradition to stop by the candy store so she can get a bag full of multiflavored jelly beans. She then picks out the white jelly beans, one by one, and hands them to me. She gets such a delight in giving me a little something that she knows I like. Lately, I've noticed that she selects more of the white jelly beans when she scoops the multiflavored collection into her bag so she can have more to hand me. Dana's willingness to share what she enjoys with me, just to see me happy, is her way of saying that she loves me.

Just as Dana enjoys doing the dishes for me, drawing pictures for me, and sharing her jelly beans with me—just to please me—there are certain things I will do for her and my husband simply to see them smile. Whether it's making sugar cookies for Dana or cooking up a nachos supper for Hugh, I do those things because I love them and want to see them pleased.

SHOWING, NOT TELLING

We enjoy pleasing the ones we love. It's a way of *showing* them our love, instead of just talking about it. When my husband tells me—and others—that I'm the most important person in his life and yet fails to make any time for me, I begin to doubt his words. I want him to *show me* with his actions, his lifestyle, his daily choices, that I am his priority. When he leaves work on some of his busiest days to take me to lunch simply so we can spend some time together, or when he writes out a card to tell me he was thinking about me, it reaffirms to me that he does mean what he says. The little things—like jelly beans, lunch dates, and nice notes—often show that we *really* love someone.

Establishing intimacy with the Lord works the same way. I can tell God, in prayer, that I love Him. And I can tell others that my relationship with Him is my top priority. But God looks at my actions, my lifestyle, my daily choices, as evidence of my love for Him and as proof that He is a priority in my life. Even the little things I do will show whether or not I *really do* love Him.

We talked in the first section of this book about all that God does to show His love for us. He pursues us, He loves and accepts us unconditionally, He sticks at our sides, promising to never leave us, He sees us as beautiful when we're in right relationship with His Son, Jesus. We've seen how He's approachable and how He's the best, most loving friend we could ever find. What then, is our response to Him? What can we do to show Him our love?

Probably by now you've been showing Him in little ways that you trust His acceptance of you, that you're resting in His security, that you're willing to rise early and present yourself before Him and look into His mirror so He can be truly pleased with you. You may be approaching Him more often with whatever is on your mind. And you may be making a sincere effort to be best friends with Him. But the point at which your relationship with Him takes flight and prepares to go the distance is the point at which you decide to become all that He desires.

In any relationship—whether it be with your parents, husband, boyfriend, children, or friends—the more you get to know someone and love that person and grow in your intimacy, the more you want to please that person and ultimately become what they desire in a daughter, wife, mother, lover, or friend. Likewise, the more you grow in your knowledge and love for the Lord, the more you will want to please Him and long to be what He desires.

HIS DESIRE FOR US

There are certain characteristics that God desires in us for our intimacy with Him to grow. But He doesn't expect us to have those characteristics already, or get them overnight. Part of His commitment to us when He invited us to be intimate with Him was that He would make you and me into the kind of women He envisions us to be.

You can probably think of a relationship or two that helped you become a better person. My father showed me how to be responsible. My mother showed me how to be spontaneous and have fun. My friend, Joan, showed me the joy of living fully for the Lord. My husband has shown me the importance of studying God's Word. Well, that's the kind of relationship you and I can enjoy with the Lord. As we grow together and discover what He desires, He will help us each become the kind of woman who epitomizes all that He wants. (And when you become what God wants for you, you are becoming the best woman you can be.) As you develop into what He desires, you will experience the true fulfillment that intimacy with God can bring.

THINK ABOUT IT

When you think about pleasing God, what comes to mind? Do you think in terms of sacrifice and giving something up for Him? Do you think of exercising spiritual disciplines like praying, studying the Word, talking of your faith to others? What do you do to show the Lord that you *really* love Him?

I mentioned in the first chapter of this book that intimacy with God involves learning what He loves and clinging to it and knowing what He hates and avoiding it at all costs. Being able to please, and avoid disappointing the one we love, is essential in *any* relationship to foster intimacy and trust. As we begin pleasing God by doing—and being—all that He desires, we develop a deeper level of intimacy with the Lord. To please God, then, we must know exactly what it is that thrills His heart.

God tells us clearly what He desires in the pages of His written Word. All I have to do is read His book and I can know what He loves and what He hates, what types of things please Him and what disappoints Him. I can be very sure of what thrills Him and what breaks His heart. In this chapter, we'll focus on the things that God loves and how to cling to them (and in the next chapter, we'll look at the things that God hates and how to avoid them).

A STATE OF THE HEART

Throughout the Old Testament, we read of men who thrilled the Lord's heart. David, being called a man after God's heart, was one. God praised him for being a man *who will do all My will.*[1] Job, whom God called a *blameless and upright man*, was another. (God actually bragged to Satan "Have you considered my servant Job? *For there is no one like him on the earth*" [emphasis added].)[2]

But what about the women who caught God's eye and heart? In the New Testament I find three, all named Mary, who were singled out by God as being close to His heart: Mary, the mother of Jesus, who was called *favored one;*[3] Mary Magdalene, who showed true devotion to the Lord; and Mary of Bethany, who touched Jesus' heart in some memorable moments. In these three women who got up close and personal with Jesus, I see a *submissive* heart, a *devoted* heart, and a *passionate* heart.

A submissive heart

Mary, Jesus' mother, showed an extremely submissive heart. While still a young teenager, she was told by an angel of God that she would bear the long-awaited Messiah. Although she risked public ridicule and death if her people discovered she was pregnant and unmarried, the young Mary trusted God and His plan for her protection. Whatever dreams she and Joseph may have planned for their life together were thrown to the wind the day she received the startling news about her future. And although she stepped into an extremely difficult, demanding, and ultimately agonizing role as the mother of the One who would bear the sins of the world, Mary responded to the news with the words, "I am the Lord's servant.... May it be to me as you have said" (Luke 1:38 NIV). Wow! No reservations here. No apparent wavering or, "I'll get back to you on that." Mary had a submissive heart that was willing to do whatever her Lord had asked of her. And that heart found favor with God.

A devoted heart

Mary Magdalene had only known a life of torment before Jesus freed her from the bondage of seven demons. The new life she had was spent in devotion to the One who had set her free. She was one of the women who followed Jesus and His disciples, enthusiastically giving of her time and money to help in Jesus' ministry.[4] On the night Jesus was arrested, all of His disciples deserted Him. But not Mary Magdalene. She followed Jesus and His cross through the streets of Jerusalem and all the way up to Calvary. She witnessed the excruciating pain that Jesus endured as He was nailed to and hung from that cross. This woman huddled, crying, with two other women at the foot of Jesus' cross and felt the pain as her Lord was being crucified.[5] Even after Jesus died, Mary would not leave Him. She stayed and assisted the men who took His bloody body off the cross and prepared it for burial. And when Jesus was sealed inside a tomb, she lingered still.[6] Later, after the Sabbath, Mary rose early to return to the tomb to complete the hasty preparations that had been made on Jesus' body two nights earlier. (Perhaps she intended to roll that huge stone back by herself in an attempt to get to her precious Lord in the tomb.) The Lord was evidently aware of her unwavering devotion and chose to appear to *her* first, before anyone else.[7]

Mary Magdalene, this woman who knew so well the meaning of grace, was the first one to hear Jesus speak after He arose (She was so excited Jesus had to keep her from clinging to Him). And Jesus entrusted her with being the first to proclaim the glorious news of His resurrection. Mary's loyalty and devotion was recognized by Jesus, and her devotion to Him didn't diminish, even in His death. Mary Magdalene had a devoted heart, and it drew her closer to the heart of God.

A passionate heart

Mary of Bethany, the sister of Martha and Lazarus, had a passionate heart toward the Lord Jesus. In the accounts we read of her, we see that she loved Jesus passionately—so much that she neglected the work at hand in order to sit at His feet and hang on His every word,[8] so much that she ran and fell at His feet and poured out her heart to Him after her brother had died. The Bible tells us that when Jesus saw her crying at His feet, He was deeply moved and cried with her.[9] Mary's presence at Jesus' feet once again touched His heart as she, shortly before Jesus' death, anointed him with an expensive perfume and dried His feet with her own hair. By taking what could have been the most valuable thing she owned and using it to anoint the head and body of Jesus, Mary showed a passion for loving God with all she had and for seizing the moment to revel in His presence.[10] Mary's passion for the Lord was such that Jesus said wherever the gospel is preached, the story of her devotion would be told in memory of her.[11] Mary of Bethany had a passionate heart, and it drew her closer to Jesus.

GOD'S LOVE LIST

I really want to be one of those people whom God singles out and speaks highly of. I want to grab hold of His heart in a way no one else ever has. I want Him to stop the angels in heaven and say, "Have you noticed my servant, Cindi? There is no one like her in all the earth." I love Him, so I want to please Him.

If you share with me that desire (and you must, because you've come with me this far), then let's look together at what we can do to be women who please God and touch His heart.

One of the Old Testament prophets told us what the Lord *requires* of us: "to do justice, to love kindness and to walk humbly with your God" (Micah 6:8). And we can be certain that He desires for us to do these things with a heart that is submissive, devoted, and passionate. In other words, by doing with *all our heart* what He *requires*, we will ultimately be doing what He *desires*.

He desires first place in our lives

First of all, God desires to be first of all. He not only desires it, He *deserves* it. We must be careful not to relegate God to a small corner of our lives and take Him out and use Him when it's convenient and when we have the time. God wants to be the most important person in our lives. He desires to be first every day and in every way.

He desires obedience

Another biggie with God is that we obey Him. He *requires* that we obey Him and He *desires* that we do it with a willing heart. He says in His Word that to obey Him is better than any sacrifice we can offer or gift we can give Him (1 Samuel 15:22). Jesus said in John 14:15, "If you love Me, you will keep My commandments." Notice Jesus didn't expect *everyone* to obey Him—only those who *loved* Him, only those who were His. Our obedience is evidence of our love for Him. So obeying Him with a heart that says, "I love you" is something He truly desires.

He desires our total dependence on Him

It is an insult to God when we think we can take care of ourselves. We cannot be saved from our sin situation without Him. We cannot live a holy life without Him. We can't do much of anything without Him. Jesus said in John 15:5 that apart from Him we can do *nothing*. He was referring to our attempts to live a good Christian life apart from His enabling spirit.

My husband wants me to depend on him to fix things around the house, make wise decisions on behalf of our family, and provide what we need financially. In fact, he *enjoys* providing for his wife and daughter. Likewise, my Heavenly Husband wants me to depend on Him for everything I need.

He desires faith

Hebrews 11:6 says, "Without faith it is impossible to please Him." Faith means relying on God and the unseen things about Him and not on the things we can see.[12] Faith means taking God at His Word. It means believing He can do the impossible. Faith goes hand in hand with depending on Him.

My husband wants our daughter, Dana, to believe he can do *anything*. It's part of the pride that I think every father has toward his children. He wants to be her hero. God is my hero—and yours, too. Jesus said nothing was impossible for Him (Matthew 19:26). Do you really believe that? If so, you are delighting His heart.

He desires humility

In Psalm 51:17, a repentant David tells us that God desires a "broken and contrite heart." Surely a man after God's own heart knew what God desired. God wants to see in us a humility and brokenness that is truly sorry for our sin, that admits we are not the all-in-all, and that sees Him as the One who enables us to do all that we are able to do.

Our English word *contrite* comes from the Latin word *conterere*, which means "to crush."[13] God wants us to be absolutely crushed when we disappoint or offend Him in any way. A woman with a contrite (or crushed) heart is tender and sensitive toward the one she loves. So she will live with a heart that is careful not to disappoint, offend, or let down the one she loves the most. The New Testament tells us that this kind of humility, this kind of gentle and quiet spirit, is "precious in the sight of God" (1 Peter 3:3-4).

He desires loyalty

Hosea 6:6 says that God delights "in loyalty rather than sacrifice, and in the knowledge of God rather than burnt offerings." God desires that we know Him because He knows that when we truly understand who He is, we will love Him. And when we know Him and love Him, He delights in our loyalty. To have loyalty for someone or something is to have "feelings of devoted attachment and affection."[14] God wants our wholehearted devotion.

God told Moses He was a jealous God (Exodus 20:5). In fact, He even said His *name* was Jealous (Exodus 34:14), implying that was a major identifying characteristic of His. Our Heavenly Husband doesn't want us to give Him only part of us and leave the rest (or the best) for someone else. He desires to have us all for Himself. He wants you—heart, soul, mind, and body. Are you all His? Or are you dividing your heart with someone or something else?

He desires sincerity

Psalm 51:6 says God desires truth in the innermost being. David, who knew well the heart of God, tells us that our honesty, vulnerability, and willingness to place everything before the Lord is what God desires. That's because honesty and sincerity are necessary for intimacy to exist. Having truth in our innermost being means we are without a stained conscience. We are honest before God, every morning and every night. It also means we are honest with ourselves when it comes to where we are in our relationship with Him and where we'd *like* to be. I know many Christians who'd like to believe their relationship with Christ goes deeper than it really does. They do all the right things: pray every night before bed, attend church every Sunday, give the correct answers at Bible study. But they have no passion for the Lord. Nothing shakes them to the core when they consider their love for Him. They aren't hot for the Lord. Having sincerity and truth in your innermost being means getting honest about how much you really are committed to God and what you're willing to change, add, or get rid of so that your actions match your desire.

He desires a grateful heart

Throughout the Psalms, we are told to give thanks to God with a heart full of gratitude. Psalm 92:1 says, "It is good to give thanks to the LORD." Why? Because it keeps us humble. Because it keeps us focused on the giver, not ourselves, the recipient. Because it keeps us in the mind-set that we don't necessarily deserve all we get and therefore, someone else, be it God or another person, is deserving of thanks and praise. Colossians 2:6-7 says that if we have received Jesus Christ, we should walk in Him by being people "overflowing with gratitude." Graciousness keeps us with a broken and contrite heart (which we looked at earlier).

He desires generosity

The Bible says God loves a cheerful giver.[15] He wants us to give to Him and others liberally. He wants us to give of our time, resources, money, and heart. At times I'm not a very generous person. My husband is. My neighbors are. And I know that I need to be. Giving liberally and without expectation of getting back is pleasing to God, and will help us to more closely relate to the kind of person Jesus was—giving of Himself liberally, fully, freely for the sacrifice of our sins.

He desires that we be more like His Son

If we took all the things that God desires of us—that we practice putting Him first, that we be obedient, dependent on Him, full of faith, humble, loyal, sincere, and gracious—we would have a picture of Jesus Christ. And that, in essence, is what pleases God. In fact, God's desire for us from the beginning of time has been to make each of us become like His Son (Romans 8:29). And when we fulfill that purpose of becoming more like Christ, God's heart is thrilled.

A PASSION FOR PLEASING HIM

Psalm 149:4 says *God delights in His people*. He has His heart's desire when we are living for Him, through Him, and in Him. What a concept—that *He* delights in us! That makes me want to please Him with all I am and all I become.

Lady Julian of England obviously wanted to please God with all that she was and all she would become. That is evident in a prayer she wrote more than 600 years ago. She prayed that God would give her three wounds: the wound of *contrition* (to be truly sorry for her sins); the wound of *compassion* (to be hurt by the pain she saw in others); and the wound of *longing after God* (to long for His return so badly it hurt). Those three wounds that God ended up giving her pierced her heart and showed her Lord that she was painfully passionate about pleasing Him, living for Him, loving Him.

WHAT ABOUT YOU?

Could you pray as Lady Julian did? Could I? We could—and would—if we truly wanted to give Him all that He desires—if we truly wanted to *be* His delight and desire.

Psalm 37:4 exhorts us to delight ourselves in the Lord, and He will give us the desires of our heart. I've found that to delight myself in the Lord makes Him *become* my desire, and therefore I have all that I want. Nothing pleases God more than when we delight in Him.

We can delight God by:

1. *Delighting in His Word*

Study it, memorize it, meditate on it, and love to live it. A woman who delights in the Word of God speaks it to just about everyone she comes in contact with. That's because she not only knows it so well, but she loves it. She loves to repeat it, reflect on it, teach it to others, and talk about it. A woman who delights in the Word never needs to tell people she loves God's Word. It shows through her lifestyle, her actions, her daily choices. David prayed in Psalm 19:14, "Let the words of my mouth and the meditation of my heart be acceptable in Thy sight." When our words are His Word and our meditations are on His Word, we know they are acceptable and pleasing to Him. And we know that He is delighted.

2. Delighting in His Presence

David said, "In Thy presence is fullness of joy" (Psalm 16:11). Do you feel complete joy in the presence of God? Do you love everything about being with Him, including being with His people, praising Him in the presence of others, spending time in prayer with Him? God loves your communion. So delighting in His presence will allow the two of you to grow together in what you both most enjoy.

Now, delighting in His presence doesn't mean that you're always happy with your circumstances. It means, rather, that you're always aware of His presence—that is what gives you joy. We can experience joy even in the dark times when life is difficult because we strongly sense the presence and peace of God. Delighting in His presence is something we can do no matter what our circumstances because He always goes through them with us.

3. Delighting in Him

In one of his psalms, David prayed, "My soul waits in silence for *God only*; from Him is my salvation. *He only* is my rock and my salvation, my stronghold; I shall not be greatly shaken" (Psalm 62:1-2, emphasis added). Are you waiting for, longing for, living for *God only*? When *God only* is all you seek, you will know what it means to delight in the Lord and become what He desires.

When we truly delight in God, it will show in our actions, our lifestyle, our daily choices: We will make time for Him, seek to know everything there is to know about Him, experience joy in His presence, sing with a heart full of gratitude, long to be in His presence during prayer, and speak often of His wonders and His ways.

LIVING IT OUT

Do you desire the Lord enough to delight in Him...to make Him the source of all that you long for? Do you love Him enough to give Him what He wants of *you* and your life? Do you want to have a heart that is submissive, devoted, and passionate? If you can answer yes to any of those questions, you are on your way to becoming a woman who knows God intimately, a woman who has discovered what He desires, a woman who—in God's eyes—stands out from the rest.

Go ahead—tell Him how you long to give Him what He desires. He wants nothing more than to take you in His arms and show you how *you* can be the desire of His heart.

Becoming What He Desires

The more you are aware of God's desires, the more you can cling to them. Here are some things you can do to discover what thrills the heart of God. And as you work through them, you will be putting yourself in a position where He can mold and shape you into the kind of woman He has always wanted:

1. Read Micah 6:8-9. List at least one or two ways that you can do the following this week:
- Exercise justice
- Love mercy
- Walk humbly before God

2. Think of three qualities you desire most from someone in an intimate relationship. (Remember, don't think of qualities that are expected. Think of what you'd truly desire.) Now, commit yourself to cultivating those qualities in yourself for the benefit of your True Love, the Lord Jesus.

3. Read Psalm 37:4. Explain what you think it means to *delight yourself* in the Lord. What desires do you believe He has placed in your heart as a result of delighting in Him?

4. In what areas of your relationship with God do you need to have...

- a more submissive heart?
- a more devoted heart?
- a more passionate heart?

5. Consider praying Lady Julian's prayer. What would it mean to you to have...
- the wound of contrition?
- the wound of compassion?
- the wound of longing after God?

8
Avoiding What He Dislikes

I remember the time I turned my back on God. It didn't happen all at once and it certainly wasn't anything I had planned. But before I realized it, my heart was hardened, intimacy with God was lost, and I came face to face with my fallen nature.

I was a junior in college and had just been betrayed by my Christian boyfriend. My heart was broken, but I was determined that I could go on, because never again would I let someone else become more important to me than God. I had been studying the Proverbs, and so I was feeling very wise, and very strong, spiritually, despite my recent emotional upset. But I forgot that pride goes before the fall.

I had noticed a mutual attraction between myself and one of the young men on the university's newspaper staff. Because I was the only Christian on the editorial staff (among four young men), I believed God put me there to be light in these students' darkness and to stand boldly for my faith. But my Christian beliefs were more of a novelty to this one young man, and as he flirted with me and mocked my faith, I foolishly began to flirt back. I didn't realize I was flirting with danger.

Although this man was very antagonistic toward God, I believed I could use his interest in me to influence his life and draw him closer to God. I started dating him and told myself that as long as I held to my values and as long as he understood that I would never budge when it came to my beliefs, that *I* would be the one to influence *him*.

The more I began to see this man, the more I was becoming someone I didn't know anymore. I can't remember exactly how it happened, but little by little I became less sensitive to God's voice and more sensitive to this man's. I began going places I wouldn't have frequented before. I began entertaining thoughts and having conversations that before would never have entered my mind or exited my mouth. Gradually, the things I was so sure I wouldn't budge on began to shift from underneath me. I remember finding it difficult to pray and finding it easy to rationalize dating a man who didn't share my convictions. As the weeks went by and my heart continued to be divided, I began to think less and less of the Shepherd of my heart and turned more of my thoughts and energy toward pleasing this man. I began to believe that I was in love with him, and with that feeling came a deaf ear to the still small voice of conviction that had been tugging at my heart.

By the time a few months had gone by, I was going through the motions in my Christian life, attending church on Sundays and reading token verses in my Bible, but avoiding any serious time alone with God or with Christian friends who might ask about my personal life. To others I seemed to be doing fine spiritually, and whenever I began to feel like I was living a lie, I justified my feelings of guilt by telling myself that I had a right to be treated well and the last Christian guy I dated had treated me far worse than this unbeliever.

About four months into my "wandering," I was driving home from a friend's house on a rainy night. I remember not being able to see well through the wet, blurry windshield, even though the wipers were working at top speed. I began to panic when I realized for a second that I didn't know where I was heading. I immediately pulled the car off the side of the road and shut off the engine. Staring out the windshield at the darkness and confusion, I realized that I didn't know where I was—or who I was— any longer.

From the time I was a child, I identified myself as someone who loved Jesus. As a young teenager, I defined who I was by what I believed and how it differed from the rest of the world. Now, at 21 and wandering free, I felt lost. *I am what I believe, but what do I believe?* I asked myself. *If I'm not a follower of Christ, who am I?* I had definitely not been following in the Lord's footsteps, but cutting a new, unfamiliar path that followed my own desires.

I began to cry uncontrollably as I realized that I was gradually becoming everything I never wanted to be. But most devastating to me in that dark, scary moment was the fact that I had turned my back on my One True Love, and I suddenly felt the lonely, despairing feeling that comes with the loss of intimacy. My heart had been racing in a different direction after someone else. And without realizing it, I had allowed a wandering heart to grow hardened and heavy until it had become insensitive to the delicate bond of intimacy I had shared with God most of my life.

I sat in my car, alongside the road in the rain, for about an hour, crying my eyes out. Vivid pictures of my disobedience and compromise flooded my mind, and I was ready to turn back around and head home.

"God, I don't know where I'm going anymore," I cried out with an anguished heart. "It's so dark and I feel so alone out here. I'm sorry for going out on my own, away from You. Please lead me back to You, where I feel safe and secure. Please show me the way back home."

As I started the car again, the rain began to clear. I did a U-turn in the middle of the street and started heading back home. When I arrived at my apartment, I ran into my bedroom, got down on my knees, and asked God for a new heart—one that would never leave Him again. I vowed that night to never again go down that dark road of disobedience. And I never spoke to that man again, either.

That experience of going out on my own and letting my heart grow cold toward God has made me determined to never let my heart harden against Him again. Oh, I still disappoint Him at times, but I must be careful to come back to Him and confess each time that I do so my heart won't become dulled and insensitive to His call to return. If I ignore His prodding—His gentle tap upon my heart when I have done something to interrupt our intimacy—I will find myself heading again down the dark road of disobedience where the heart becomes hardened and intimacy is lost. If you've ever been down that road yourself, I'm sure you'll agree with me that it's a place you don't want to revisit.

BREAKING THE BOND OF INTIMACY

Breaking our bond of intimacy with God often happens before we even realize it. It's a gradual sin-upon-sin descent that leaves the heart insensitive to the Spirit's prodding and leaves our ears deaf to the Spirit's call to return. None of us sets out to wander from the Lover of our soul. But we all have a fallen nature, a propensity toward sin, a tendency to wander off on our own or turn our backs on God and become someone we never would've expected.

If you think this will never happen to you, I want to caution you with this one thought: If it can happen to David, a man after God's own heart, it can happen to you.

David, who was known for his sensitivity and his great love for God, went through a time in his life when he allowed his heart to wander to the point where it became hardened and callused and no longer responsive to God's voice. The year that David spent in rebellion to God may seem trivial considering he had been close to God for nearly his whole life, but the consequences of his disobedience during that one year forever changed the course of his life, his family, and his kingdom.

What made David, a man of God, allow himself to fall deeper and deeper into sin and farther away from God? We can better understand it, I think, by tracing David's steps, considering his thoughts, and examining his trip down the dark road of disobedience.

DAVID'S DARK PATH

We don't know why David stayed home when his army went out to battle the Ammonites. Perhaps he was restless; perhaps he was bored. Or maybe he was just tired from fighting so many battles that he felt he deserved a break. Whatever the reason, David's restlessness or inability to sleep caused him to wander—in many ways. He started his wandering on the roof of the palace—in the cool of the evening—and saw what he shouldn't have seen. Bathsheba, a woman who lived near the palace, was bathing on her roof. David already had some wives, but he was captivated by this woman's beauty and wanted her. He couldn't get her out of his mind.

When David asked around, he found out she was married—not to just anybody, but to Uriah, one of his best soldiers (who was at war with the rest of the army). Common sense should have set in at that point. But perhaps David wasn't listening to the voice of reason, or the soft voice of conviction in his heart. He let an innocent glance turn into a longing gaze. The gaze turned into a fantasy and then a quest. It would soon become a one-night stand. Instead of turning away from the temptation that happened to appear before him, he pursued it. David ordered Bathsheba to his palace and, apparently shutting out any thought of consequences or responsibilities, he spent the night with her.

The next morning, when Bathsheba left, perhaps David felt a little guilty. But evidently he justified his sin and his feelings, for we see no remorse. Maybe he thought to himself, *I really needed some time with someone who didn't know me, so I could rediscover who I was, away from the people and pressures of my kingdom. Bathsheba was lonely. I'm the one who sent her husband off to war, so the least I could do was comfort her in his absence. I felt somehow responsible for her. And I did treat her well in my presence.* David may have pondered the time he shared with Bathsheba and considered it a blessing, something the Lord allowed him as king. Or, he might not have thought about it at all, and continued onward with life as usual, ignoring the Spirit's prodding to confess what he had done. The bottom line was that no one else needed to know.

About a month later, David received devastating news. Bathsheba was pregnant! David hadn't planned on such a complication. *Would she talk? Would she reveal what happened? Would she be killed for her unfaithfulness to her husband?* David obviously felt he had to protect her—and himself. *I'll fix this. I'll make this right.*

David immediately called Bathsheba's husband, Uriah, home from war. He asked him about the battle, then sent him away with a gift, telling him to go home and make love to his wife. But David's soldier was so dedicated to the king's cause that he refused to go home that night and be with his wife while his fellow soldiers were at war. Instead, he slept on the king's doorstep.

David panicked when he saw his plan wasn't working. He then invited Uriah to have dinner with him and made sure Uriah drank heavily. Again David told Uriah to go home and sleep with his wife. But again, Uriah slept at David's door.

Again, David's plan had backfired. Now he was furious! If Uriah wouldn't cooperate, he would be eliminated. David wrote orders for Uriah to be taken to the front lines and left to die in the heat of battle. Little did Uriah know that the sealed message he took back to the battle commander called for his own death. And when David heard that his faithful soldier, Uriah, was indeed killed, the same man who wailed over King Saul's death didn't even shed a tear of remorse for Uriah. Perhaps that's because David had other things on his mind.

David must have watched the calendar, calculating the proper time for Bathsheba to mourn her husband's death, so he could marry her quickly and make it look like their baby was legitimate. *When would she become visibly pregnant? I'm running out of time.* When the proper time came, David married Bathsheba. During the long months that Bathsheba was pregnant and living with David, God must've been tugging at David's heart. But David's heart had grown hard. Perhaps he wasn't listening anymore.

When Bathsheba finally gave birth to their son, no one questioned it. Nothing was said. David must've breathed a sigh of relief when it appeared that his tracks were covered. *It's done. Now back to kingdom business.*

But God didn't forget what had happened. About a year after David first looked at Bathsheba, God sent a prophet, Nathan, to straighten David out. David had stopped listening to the Holy Spirit and the conviction of his own heart, so God had to take a more direct approach.

He had Nathan tell David about a man who had committed a horrible sin. Nathan then asked the king what he should do to punish the man. And David, who was insensitive to the condition of his own heart, didn't recognize himself as the villain in Nathan's story.

"*You* are the man!" Nathan said, looking David straight in the eyes. And David's eyes, which once had looked to God above anything or anyone else, opened to see the hardened, callused sinner he had become!

Feeling the depths to which he had sunk in his relationship with God, David cried out in anguish, "Create in me a pure heart, O God, and renew a steadfast spirit within me. Do not cast me from Thy presence or take Thy Holy Spirit from me."[1] Upon seeing how crushed David was over his sin, God forgave him and restored the relationship. But David didn't escape the consequences of his season of sin. God took the life of David and Bathsheba's baby and cursed David's house, promising that the adultery and conspiracy he had committed toward Uriah would come back around to haunt him. David, his wives, his children, and his kingdom all felt the effects of this punishment.

Perhaps the most devastating consequence of David's wandering, however, was the loss of intimacy between him and his Lord, whom he had loved and pleased since he was a child.[2]

David must have felt the loss of that closeness with the Lord to pray, "Do not cast me from Thy presence." David's God, the same as ours, is one who never leaves. But because David had done something God hated, their bond of fellowship was severed, the relationship was damaged, the intimacy was lost. We can only wonder if their intimacy was ever again the same as it was before the man after God's own heart had broken God's heart.

ESTABLISHING CAUTION

Intimacy with God takes too long to establish to lose it over careless living. And so often, we disappoint God through carelessness, through simply not realizing the seriousness of certain offenses against Him. We must be so cautious, my friend, to avoid the things that can tear through the intimacy we have established with God. We never want to get to that restless state where we start wandering, glancing around at what we don't have and what we would really like to have. We never want to put ourselves in a position where we begin to rationalize, justify, and crowd out the conviction of God to where we cannot even see our own sin. We don't want to wake up one morning and discover we are miles away from where we want to be with God. So we must start by knowing what to avoid. That will help protect the intimacy we have with the Lover of our soul.

In the last chapter we looked at the kind of heart that would draw us closer to the Lord—an obedient, submissive, and passionate heart. We also looked at "God's Love List"—the characteristics and things that, when done with an obedient, submissive, and passionate heart, will make us the kind of women God truly desires.

Now let's look at "God's Hate List" and the things that develop a heart that is disobedient, hardened, and complacent. When we are aware of the things that cause us to drift from Him, we can avoid them altogether or at least confess them and return to our loving, accepting, ever-present, and always approachable God and let Him renew a right spirit within us.

GOD'S HATE LIST

Solomon, David's son, describes in the sixth chapter of Proverbs the things that God hates. (Perhaps he learned of them from his father.) He describes them, body part by body part, to indicate how offensive it is to God when we use anything He has given us in a way that is not glorifying to Him. One writer paraphrases Proverbs 6:16-19 like this:

> Here are six things God hates, and one
> more that he loathes with a passion:
> eyes that are arrogant,
> a tongue that lies,
> hands that murder the innocent,
> a heart that hatches evil plots,
> feet that race down a wicked track,
> a mouth that lies under oath,
> a troublemaker in the family.[3]

At first glance, we might assume that we aren't guilty of any of those things. But let's take a closer look at them, under different names, and see if there are any that may be affecting our intimacy with God.

Pride

A word that sums up "arrogant" or "haughty" eyes is *pride*. God hates pride, and I can guess why. It was pride that caused Satan to want to be like God and therefore be cast out of heaven, taking a third of the angels with him.[4] It was pride that caused Adam and Eve to want to be like God and be cursed with sin in the human race.[5] It was pride that caused Moses to strike a rock and not treat God reverently and thus be kept from entering the promised land.[6] And it is pride that keeps you and me from yielding our entire selves to the One who died for us.

Pride manifests itself in several ways, the most common being an insistence that we can take care of ourselves. Pride is also when we say, "I'm better than you," "I deserve this," or, "I'm good at this." It could be, "Hey, look at me!"—calling attention to ourselves, or having to be the one in the spotlight.

In the last chapter we learned that God desires for us to be totally dependent upon Him. Pride says, "I don't need God—or anyone else." Sometimes it says, "I'm strong enough to handle this" (remember my situation?) or, "God should've given me more" (remember David's situation?). Pride is destructive to a relationship with God. And it is something that God hates.

Deceit

A lying tongue is another characteristic that God hates. God desires truth in the innermost being, so He despises deceit in any form. When a couple named Ananias and Sapphira lied to the leaders of the early church about the price for which they sold a piece of land, God struck them dead.[7] Now that seems rather severe! Yet God needed to make a serious point to the early church: that truth and integrity would reign, and dishonesty would not be tolerated in any form. We may think theirs was a more serious lie, but *all* lying is serious to God—even the little white lies or the times we merely omit the truth. When we lie, we distance ourselves from people, we give Satan a foothold in our lives, we give opportunity for others to question our integrity, and we hurt the bond of intimacy between us and God. When we lie to our spouse, we distance ourselves from him. When we lie to our children, they lose faith in us. When we lie to God, we affect our relationship with Him as well.

Destroying others

Murdering the innocent or shedding innocent blood with our hands (Proverbs 6:17) may sound like something we have never done. But any time we hurt or destroy another person we have, in a sense, shed innocent blood.

And it isn't something we do with just our hands. Destroying another person can be done with our eyes, mouth, and feet as well. Have your eyes ever destroyed someone with a look that kills? Have your words devastated a person's confidence, reputation, or feelings? How many times have your feet taken you—or someone else—to places where you shouldn't have been or where you've caused someone else to fall spiritually? Destroying others—whether physically, emotionally, or spiritually—is a serious offense to God.

Scheming

A heart that hatches evil plans or devises wicked schemes is neither an obedient heart nor a submissive heart. It is a heart that seeks revenge and satisfies self. David schemed against Uriah as God looked on. God's desire is that we leave matters concerning other people in His very capable hands and leave our hearts bearing all things, believing all things, hoping all things, and enduring all things.[8] When you mentally scheme against another person, you may think it's harmless and therefore it's not really a sin, but every action in our life starts in our mind. What we think about, we eventually do. And Jesus said thinking about sin is the same as committing it.

Racing toward evil

Feet that run rapidly to evil or race down the track toward something other than God are feet that are anxious to disobey. David let his feet (and his heart) run toward an opportunity to be with Bathsheba instead of staying on a course directed toward God and obedience to His laws. Then David let his feet do whatever was necessary to cover his tracks, instead of running back to God and confessing his sin and letting God work out the aftermath.

Sometimes we're passionate about doing the wrong

things. We want so badly to have something we shouldn't or we obsess over something or someone other than God. When that happens we are running toward the wrong things—things that lead us away from a deeper, closer walk (and run) with God. God wants us, like Mary of Bethany, to have a heart that is passionate for *Him*—for hearing *His* word, for sitting in *His* presence, for giving to *Him* of all that we have. Passion for anything other than God is putting something else before Him. And God *hates* that.

For many women, obsession is a very real problem. I once was in a home that was filled with antique and porcelain dolls. For fun, my daughter and I began counting them. We found nearly 50 in the living room alone! They sat on the couch, the chairs, the fireplace, the mantel, and even around the kitchen table. (In fact, the family sat on stools at the kitchen counter to eat dinner so the dolls weren't disturbed from their places around the table.) The dolls were lovely...there were just so many of them. The last I heard, this woman was still buying more dolls for her home. Many of us collect things we like, but when we let those things dominate our time and our thoughts and our space and they control us, rather than us controlling them, they have become an obsession.

We can obsess over more than just things. Some women obsess over neatness, over cleanliness and avoiding germs, over their looks or their houses or their husbands or their children. Whatever we pour our heart into, whatever occupies our thoughts and desires, whatever becomes a priority in our life over that of loving God, is something we obsess over. This is also considered unfaithfulness because putting *anything* (food, things, friendships, dating relationships, fiancée or husband, children, job, career, success) higher than God on our list of desires turns that thing (or person) into a god that we seek. God is a jealous God. He hates when we run toward, obsess after, or seek for *anything* other than Him.

Lying under oath

Just as God hates deceit and a lying tongue, He hates a false witness or a misrepresentation or an exaggeration of another person or situation. Lying under oath is not only misrepresentation, but it involves withholding from someone else—or God—what is due them. Making promises to God—or anyone else—that we are unable to keep can be a form of "lying under oath." God desires that we be women of integrity, and that means He desires that we be honest in all our dealings and verbal accounts and that we be careful not to misrepresent anyone or anything.

Spreading dissension

God hates it when there are divisions among people, especially in the family of God. Many of us have experienced disputes with family members; that's pretty much inevitable. But disputes among brothers and sisters in Christ is something that we shouldn't tolerate or be involved with. As a minister's wife, I've seen many times, in my church as well as in others, the pain and trouble that results from a single person who has a complaint and then tells other people that complaint one by one, and then before you know it, that person has rallied the troops, spreading dissension throughout the family of God. Most of the time the initial complaint was so petty it becomes forgotten in the midst of the ensuing war. Criticism, pessimism, backbiting, and dissension are contagious, especially when they start in the church. I think that's because Satan gets a foothold in a complaint or irritation and then runs with it, like a scared fox with a fiery bush attached to its tail.

But that doesn't mean God tolerates it. God loves His church, His bride. And when we spread dissension by airing our gripes, backbiting, or leading an ill cause, we invoke His wrath. David prayed in Psalm 35:1, "Contend, O LORD, with those who contend with me: fight against those who fight against me." God *will* contend with those who fight against His people, His church, His loved ones. Don't be one who contends with God's people and thus takes on God. Be a peacemaker instead. Nip the complainer in the bud, and see how love covers a multitude of sins (James 5:20).

DEALING WITH THE GRAY

The Bible spells out some things very plainly that we are to avoid, such as the things on our list from Proverbs 6. Then there are what we call the "gray areas." If we want to indulge in something questionable that the Bible doesn't address specifically, we'll say to ourselves, *Well, the Bible doesn't say I can't do that!* As my husband points out from the pulpit, some things are so obvious God doesn't need to say anything. Often the conviction of the Holy Spirit in our lives will convince us if something "gray" in our life is offensive to Him and is interfering with our intimacy with Him.

Sometimes a "gray thing" is not in itself bad. But if it keeps us from loving God completely and making Him a priority or if it interferes in any way with our time or intimacy with Him, it must go.

Over the years I have known families that would miss an occasional Sunday morning at church because of a special sports tournament their kids were a part of. I even know of a family that began to skip church frequently because of regular season games and eventually practices that were scheduled on Sunday mornings.

This "gray area," unfortunately, kept them from their Sunday morning obligations at church, prevented them from weekly corporate worship, interfered with their fellowship with God's people, and contradicted the spiritual priorities they were attempting to establish in their home. They admitted that the sports schedule had become a distraction in their spiritual life, but ultimately kept the kids on the field. Had the soccer field become more important than the sanctuary? Could one's sports life be of greater importance than one's spiritual life? If so, the "gray area" becomes not so gray anymore.

When it comes to protecting our intimacy with God, *nothing* is worth our time if it takes time away from our relationship with God. That is one way of looking at the "gray areas" of life.

If we truly want to grow with God and go the distance with Him, we will take Him seriously. Avoiding what He hates is taking God seriously. Listening to your conscience (which, in a believer, is the Holy Spirit) is taking Him seriously. Clearing out of our lives the things that distract us from pursuing Him is taking Him seriously.

THROWING IT ALL AWAY

How can we best avoid the things God hates in order to take Him seriously and continue to grow with Him in deepening intimacy? I've found a three-point plan in Philippians 3:13-14 that's very helpful for me: *"Forgetting* what lies behind and *reaching forward* to what lies ahead, I *press on* toward the goal for the prize of the upward call of God in Christ Jesus" (emphasis added).

1. *Forget about the remnants from the old life*

The old life is the one apart from intimacy with God—the life that longed for someone else to fulfill its needs; the life that lived to please itself, not God; the life that looked to worldly pleasures and momentary happiness. The old life chased after wind. When we come to know Christ and intimacy with Him, we are no longer the woman who lived for and loved things other than Him. So we need to forget about that part of our lives.

2. *Focus on what lies ahead in your intimate relationship with God*

It can only get better when you remain obedient to the Lord and put Him first. Make His love and His desires your love and your desires. By doing that, you are reaching forward to what lies ahead, the treasures upon treasures that await you in a deeply personal relationship with Christ.

3. *Forge ahead in boldly pleasing Him before any other*

Pleasing God should be considered a race. We should seek God earnestly just as a runner seeks the finish line in a race. When you forge ahead like this, you are pressing on toward the goal—total and complete intimacy with the Lover of your soul.

GETTING IT RIGHT

When you forget about your old life—as a woman seeking fulfillment everywhere else but in Christ—and focus on your new life in Him and all the possibilities, you will no doubt want to forge ahead and find the fulfillment that comes from pleasing God and remaining by His side. Living day to day by clinging to what He desires and avoiding what He hates will keep your relationship with Him alive and well. It will also keep your heart sensitive toward the Lord so you won't be as prone to wander down the road of disobedience, away from His loving embrace.

Guard your heart, my friend. Keep it open and sensitive to Him so that sin is squelched and you remain a woman bent on pleasing Him and staying safe within His loving arms.

Avoiding Interruptions to Intimacy

During our time together in this chapter, you may have thought of some actions or habits that may be interfering with your relationship with Christ. Determine through the following steps to avoid anything that comes between you and your Lord. By knowing what He hates and avoiding it at all costs, you are already taking a necessary step in growing together and preparing to go the distance with your One True Love.

1. What habit or action comes to mind when you think of something that God hates? If you can't think of anything, try to identify something—perhaps a "gray area" that may be interfering with your intimacy with the Lord. Now, in a prayer to the Lord, tell Him what you plan to do about that action or habit.

2. Think of something in particular that you may be obsessing over or running to with all your might. Write out a plan for how you will...

- forget about it
- focus on what lies ahead
- forge ahead in pleasing Him

3. Write a letter to the Lord, confessing to Him the times your heart has been disobedient, hardened, and complacent. By confessing these things, you are bringing to the altar of sacrifice the things that prevent you and Him from growing together. Keep that letter in your Bible as a reminder of your trip to the altar to sacrifice that part of your heart.

9
Listening to His Loving Voice

"What am I doing wrong?" Rita asked me with a look of exasperation in her eyes. "Why doesn't God speak to me?"

Rita had known the Lord as her Savior for a year, but she had never "heard" His voice.

"What are you expecting to hear?" I asked Rita, trying to understand where she was coming from.

"His voice, the thundering, the boom—I don't know—you tell me!" she said, throwing up her hands in frustration.

All this time that Rita had been growing in her relationship with God, she'd been waiting for God to speak audibly to her from heaven. She'd been listening for His whisper to warn her as she headed out the front door. She was watching for the burning bush, the bright lights, the vision full of crystal-clear direction. And all this time, she heard and saw nothing.

After I talked with Rita for a while about the way God speaks to His loved ones, she began to recall that God *had* spoken to her—through the counsel she received in His Word, through circumstances that led her in a certain direction, through godly advice she received from her deacon. God *had* spoken, she admitted. But she had never realized it was Him.

DISCERNING HIS VOICE

Like Rita, many of us talk to the Lord often and just want to hear our True Love speak to us now and then. But sometimes we aren't sure how He's going to do it. We're not sure what to listen for. With so much talk these days from people who claim to hear God's voice, and claim God told them this or that, it's confusing and even difficult at times to determine who it is that's speaking.

> • *A television evangelist claims to have received an order from God to start a new mission. He urges you to join in "God's work" by sending in some cash. Did he really get a message from God? Or is he a spiritual whacko with a hidden agenda?*

> • *Elizabeth has been praying for direction concerning a health problem. For the past three mornings, during her prayer time, the thought of calling a certain doctor has been going through her head. Is this God trying to tell her something or is it just a distracting thought?*

> • *Karen has been seeking direction, through prayer and Bible study, about pursuing a full-time ministry through her church. Her mother calls and happens to mention—out of the blue—that she's always envisioned Karen in some aspect of full-time ministry for the Lord. Is this confirmation from the Lord to move in that direction, or is this simply a mother's intuition at work?*

> • *You've been prayerfully considering leaving an emotionally draining career, but you don't feel you can go until God "releases" you. In your morning devotions, you stumble upon Psalm 118:5: "In my anguish I cried to the Lord, and he answered by setting me free" (NIV). Is that God's way of saying*

you have been released? Or are you twisting an application to suit your desires?

• *Ann is walking through an airport, prepared to board a flight to leave her husband. She hears her first name called out, but turns and finds no one addressing her. She continues walking, but hears her name called out again, and finally, a third time. She stops. Is this God trying to get her attention and change her mind?*

In the 30 years since I have given my life to Jesus Christ, I can probably count on one hand the times God has spoken to me in a life-changing, memorable moment. And in none of those experiences was there an audible voice, a thundering from heaven, a burning bush, or a rushing wind. It was usually a still small voice that gave me an inner peace, a loving rebuke that changed my ways, the written Word of God that pierced my heart, or a sense of calling and direction that wouldn't let me be until I followed.

God speaks in various ways by the Holy Spirit to those whom He loves—through His Word (the Bible), through prayer (and what He lays on our hearts to pray for), through circumstances in our life, and through the church (godly advice from believers). And in my experience, I would have to say that He has spoken most clearly when I've been the most obedient, the most in need of comfort, and for the most part, not straining an ear to hear Him.

TRYING TOO HARD TO HEAR

The times that I've heard God speak have been precious, not sensational. And although I didn't expect to see a burning bush, there have been times when I, like Rita, expected something more.

I was preparing to write this chapter on listening to

God when a friend gave me a three-day prayer and reflection retreat at a monastery in the mountains of Pasadena, California. *What wonderful timing!* I thought. God must be planning to give me an incredible experience in hearing His voice so I can encourage women through this chapter in how to listen to Him.

I arrived at the retreat full of anticipation, hoping God would meet me there in His own way and in His own time.

On the first afternoon, we were asked to determine what it was we wanted to hear God say. Were we seeking direction in our lives, an answer to a question, to grow closer to Him, or to just rest in His presence? I decided I wanted God to reveal to me who I really was, away from the people and pressures in my life. I wanted Him to peel back the layers of pretenses I had built up, the images I had tried to maintain, the titles I hid behind. I wanted to see myself as He sees me—laid bare and open before Him. And I wanted His "revelation" to me to be something lasting and meaningful.

I spent an evening of preparation in the chapel, confessing any actions, attitudes, or anxieties that might prevent me from hearing God's voice. Then I went back to my small, simple room to get a good night's sleep before the next day, which would be spent entirely with God.

The next morning, I was determined to create the right setting so God would speak to me. So I decided to climb the mountain range behind the monastery. On top of that mountain, I would be able to see all of the San Fernando Valley and perhaps gain a Godlike perspective on life. I thought of Noah's experience on top of Mount Ararat as he saw God brush a beautiful rainbow across the sky and heard the Almighty proclaim His promise to never destroy the earth by flood again. I thought of Moses' experience atop Mount Sinai when he heard God's voice, saw Him handwrite the Ten Commandments, and beheld His glory. I remembered Elijah's experience atop Mount Carmel, when God rained down fire from heaven to consume an offering...and then released rains to end a three-year drought. *If I can just climb to the top of that mountain, maybe I will have a mountaintop experience, too*, I thought. But after several yards up the mountain, the thick brush scratching against my bare legs prevented me from getting any further. I attempted to climb that mountain from three different directions, each time meeting heavy brush and hearing scurrying, slithering sounds that made me think of snakes.

Frustrated at not being able to scale the mountain, I walked down near the monastery grounds and saw an old oak tree. *If I can't climb a mountain, I'll climb that tree*, I thought. After all, a short man named Zacchaeus got Jesus' attention when he climbed up a tree and Jesus ended up speaking directly to him.[1] Maybe He'd do the same for me. But, since I couldn't get past the two lower limbs and gain significant height, I jumped back down and decided to go somewhere else.

I wandered the monastery gardens, walked the 14 stations of the cross, stopping along the way to contemplate Jesus' suffering and see if He was saying anything to me. But there were only the sounds of a bird chirping and the breeze blowing through the trees.

Finally I realized that if I couldn't climb a mountain or climb a tree, I'd climb the stairs to my second-floor room and seek some solitude there. Disappointed, I sunk into an old orange chair by the window and opened my Bible. It was there—in that chair—that I remembered that during my growing-up years, I had met with God in the evenings in an old orange chair by my living room window. Later, when I moved to an apartment to attend college, I brought that old orange chair with me and it was there that God continued to meet me every morning before class as I read His Word by the window. The memory of my childhood and college days in that chair, pouring out my heart to God and sensing His presence, comforted me. It was then that God spoke to my heart with the answer I had been seeking that day. Who am I laid bare and open before Him? *I am my Beloved's and He is mine.*[2] I am someone He has always loved for some unknown reason and when everything else—the titles, the achievements, the images, the obligations—is stripped away, that's who I am left with. I am not defined by what I've done, how I live, or even where I've been. I am defined by who loves me. I realized then that what I was waiting to hear from God had been told to me all my life in the pages of His Word.

We don't need to be on a mountaintop, up a tree, or even in an old orange chair to hear the gentle, reassuring voice of the One who loves us. His words of love for us, from the pages of Scripture, echo in our hearts when we get still long enough to just listen.

WHY WE NEED HIS VOICE

As women, we want to hear a voice now and then telling us we are loved. We want communication on a regular basis to feel in touch with the ones we care about. Today, when my dad tells me, "I love you, Ceenee" over the phone, or as I'm boarding a train for home, I feel closer to him. I know my father loves me, but I still want to hear it now and then.

Likewise, we often want to hear God's voice...affirming His love for us, reaffirming His direction for our lives, interacting with us through the pages of Scripture. And listening to our Lover is important if we want to grow in our relationship with Him.

I'm always after my husband for what I call "marriage maintenance" communication. I compare regular communication in a marriage to the concept of regular maintenance on a car (now that's something he can understand and appreciate). Just as a car needs frequent oil changes and a general inspection now and then to see how it's working, relationships need maintenance, too. Our relationships—whether they be with our husband, friend, parent, or child—need regular communication, observation, and inspection to see how the relationship is working. But my husband sometimes treats our marriage like a car that gets a once-a-year engine overhaul! Hugh occasionally slips into the mode of thinking that if he spends a good hour or so baring his soul or talking about issues in our marriage, then that should keep me going for another several thousand miles!

GOD'S NOT THE SILENT TYPE

I'm so thankful God isn't the silent type. He isn't an introvert who finds it hard to express Himself. He doesn't prefer silence to the sound of our voice. And getting Him to talk is not like pulling teeth. In fact, we can read His love letters to us at any time because they're all recorded for us in the pages of His Word. When we need affirmation from Him, we will find it in His Word.

God, is this really what You want for me? Lord, are You really trying to tell me something? Will You really provide all that I need today? And when God does affirm to you what He said through His Word—through people or circumstances in your life, or by leading you to another verse of Scripture—that's Him patiently clarifying Himself so you will know it is really Him speaking to you.

THE WAY GOD SPEAKS

So if God is an excellent communicator, how exactly does He communicate? I mentioned earlier that God speaks through a variety of ways. Sometimes the ways He speaks are as different and unique as the individuals to whom He is speaking. The Lord speaks to us in different ways at different times and in different tones, sometimes saying the same thing He always says but in a way that recaptures our heart and causes us to fall deeper in love with Him.

God speaks through His Word

God often speaks to us through His Word, bringing Scripture alive before our eyes to speak to our specific need or situation. Second Timothy 3:16 says, "All Scripture is inspired by God and profitable for teaching, for reproof, for correction, for training in righteousness; that the man of God may be adequate, equipped for every good work." His Word is all these things so that we will have everything we need—even intimate communication through His gentle teaching, reproof, correction, and training of our hearts and souls. So when you read God's Word and you are enlightened, convicted, or corrected, God has spoken to you.

The Bible also says that God's Word is "living and active." "Sharper than any double-edged sword, it penetrates even to dividing soul and spirit...it judges the thoughts and attitudes of the heart" (Hebrews 4:12 NIV). When your heart is pierced and you sense God is speaking directly to you, it's probably because He is. He just touched your heart with His Word.

I specifically remember a painful time during my college years when I was questioning God about His sovereignty in some things that were happening in my family. Just about the time I felt He would never answer, His words in Isaiah 55:8-9 pierced my heart: " 'For My thoughts are not your thoughts, neither are your ways My ways,' declares the LORD. 'For as the heavens are higher than the earth, so are My ways higher than your ways, and My thoughts than your thoughts.' " Wow! God was actually telling me, in His loving way, to quit trying to figure Him out. He knew what He was doing and I needed to trust Him. That gentle rebuke from the Lord provided much comfort in my life at the time. That memory of God speaking to me, through His Word, more than 15 years ago, is as vivid as if it had happened yesterday.

But if we expect something heart-piercing and earth-shattering from God every day, we may find ourselves disappointed. Think about the daily or frequent conversations you have with friends, with co-workers, or (if you've been so blessed) with your husband. Does your husband or boyfriend or best friend say things every day that give you a warm fuzzy feeling, that make your spine tingle, and make you feel as if you've received divine direction? Not likely. If they did, after a while those shivers would disappear and you would probably take advantage of the voice you hear. God's words are there for us every day. But sometimes we take them for granted. *I've read it (or heard it) before,* we say, and quickly close our Bibles and head out the door. We need to pay careful attention at all times, for the Lord will often say the same things to us in new ways.

When someone tells you, "I love you," it may be something you've heard before, but it's a lot more meaningful when it's said with a warm touch, a bouquet of roses, or a tight hug. But for us to get that gesture, we need to spend time in that person's presence. Are you spending time in God's Word, letting Him examine your heart and reveal what you really need to hear? Or do you whip through your morning Bible-reading, hoping He'll speak quickly, before you have to shut the book and head out the door or get on with your day? Spend unhurried time with God and His Word, and as you do, you may find Him speaking to you in ways you hadn't noticed before.

God speaks through His witnesses

God's Spirit indwells those who have a relationship with Him. Therefore, God can speak to you through the wise counsel of another believer. But here we must be careful. When we sense God is speaking to us through someone else, we must ask ourselves:

- Does this contradict anything in God's Word?
- Is this something that provides peace and healing?
- Is this within the nature of God?
- Can this be backed up by Scripture or the affirmation of godly people?

I can recall many people God has spoken through to get a message across to me during various stages of my life. One was my cousin, Andy, who gave me some timely words in a gentle way that really made me think about how I was coming across to others. Another was my youth pastor, Tom, who confronted me from time to time about aspects of my character that could cause me heartache later on in life. Sometimes God speaks to us through others to convict us, reprove us, encourage us, or direct us. When He does, and we have tuned our hearts to listen, we will feel a sense of peace and rightness about what was said, even if the words are painful to hear.

God speaks through His creation

Psalm 19:1-2 says, "The heavens are telling of the glory of God; and their expanse is declaring the work of His hands. Day to day pours forth speech, and night to night reveals knowledge." This psalm tells us that God speaks through His creation—sometimes to tell us how great He is, other times to tell us how much we are loved.

God not only speaks to us through nature, but through the natural elements He created and the circumstances of life. I remember being very convinced that God was speaking during a time of national and local crisis. I was attending a large church in Southern California which prayed corporately one Sunday in the spring of 1991 for God's deliverance—for the American soldiers on the front lines of Operation Desert Storm and for the end of a drought that was consuming the land in Central and Southern California. The following week, the war in the Middle East ended victoriously for American troops, and the same day that the cease-fire was announced, the state of California was drenched in floodlike rains. I remember thinking that morning as the rain poured down and people celebrated the news of the soldiers coming home that God had opened the floodgates of heaven with blessings that were raining down on us.

Was there a connection between our prayer and the end of the war and the drought? I really can't say. I do know that God desires for men to live in peace. And God has promised to heal our lands when we gather corporately to pray (2 Chronicles 7:14). I also know that as we pray, God aligns our hearts with His so that we end up praying for things according to His will. One of the mysteries of God is that He will do what He has purposed to do, regardless of our prayers, but at the same time He desires that we pray for the things on our hearts. At least to me, and several others within that church, it seemed as if God was making a statement to the world in the amazing things that happened that week: *I am the Provider of blessings, the Giver of victories, the Supplier of rains. Any more questions?*

In chapter 3 we looked at Asaph's discouragement in Psalm 77 because he couldn't see or hear God and thought perhaps that God had deserted him. But remember, when Asaph began looking around him, he heard the voice of God in creation. "The clouds poured out water; the skies gave forth a sound; Thy arrows flashed here and there. The sound of Thy thunder was in the whirlwind" (Psalm 77:17-18). Asaph wasn't hearing anything from God personally, but when he stopped to look around and listen, he heard God's presence—and voice—everywhere.

God speaks through whispers on the heart

Sometimes we feel urged to do something and we can't explain why. Through prayer and discernment we can figure out if that is God's whisper on our heart. Sometimes God speaks to us this way through prayer, by nudging us to pray for something we wouldn't otherwise have prayed for. When God directs our prayers He is speaking to us, whispering to us words of guidance, discernment, encouragement. Sometimes we call this our conscience, or our "little voice inside." But the One who dwells within us has a voice as well. I call it my "loving voice inside." He whispers encouragement. He whispers to me suggestions for acts of love toward someone in need. He whispers words to say at the proper time to heal another's heart. When you hear your "loving voice inside," thank Him for what He spoke to you.

CULTIVATING A HEART TO HEAR

There is no sure-fire formula for hearing God speak. He speaks in His own way and in His own time to the hearts that are prepared to hear Him. But if we cultivate a heart to hear, we can be sure that His silence is not on account of our not listening.

Here are some things we can do to quiet our hearts to listen:

1. *Cut out the noise*

Michael W. Smith recorded a song in the 1980s about how we live in a "world that's wired for sound." We have so much background noise around us, from the household appliances, to blaring traffic, to the noises that get embedded in our heads. For most of us, that's normal. (The first time Hugh spent the night in my hometown, he couldn't believe how quiet it was. Kingsburg, a little village in California's Central Valley, surrounded by orchards and farmlands, was so quiet after dark that this "Bay Area boy" couldn't get to sleep. But once he did, he didn't wake until he heard the steam whistle of the 5:00 A.M. train that comes through town.) I know women who don't like it when it's too quiet and keep their televisions on for background noise, and women who cannot drive without the radio playing.

Try shutting off the television, switching off the radio, and cutting out the noise. There may be some ringing in your ears for a few minutes, but that's the sound of silence. And it's the first step to getting ready to listen. We can't expect to hear God if we're crowding Him out with other voices and sounds.

2. *Confess what's in your heart*

By confessing sin, you are eliminating the barriers in your heart and mind that may be preventing you from hearing God's voice. We looked in the last chapter at how David no longer heard God's voice because his heart had been hardened—and then callused—with sin. Sin builds a deafening ear to the voice of God. Confess not only your actions, but your attitudes and anxieties as well. When your heart and mind are cleared of any offenses against Him, you will be prepared to hear Him.

3. *Come before Him quietly*

Quietly doesn't only mean silently. It implies stillness as well. Remember David's prayer in Psalm 62:5: "My soul, wait in silence for God only." We don't know how long David had to wait, only that he waited. I imagine his waiting wasn't just done quietly, however. David had to not only be silent, but be still. Silence is external. Stillness is internal. Being quiet in the inner recesses of our heart means not worrying, not thinking of things to do, cutting out the noise in our heads as well.

Sometimes we can be refreshed by God's presence simply by being still. No words, no specific direction or command—only stillness. That is His comforting presence on our heart, His smile at our stillness, His pleasure at our rest.

4. *Consider the lilies*

Sometimes a few moments alone can cause us to look around and "smell the flowers." It was times like this, when Asaph was waiting for God to reveal Himself, that He saw Him in the clouds, rain, and wind. Times of silence and reflection give God an open channel to your heart. Maybe the only thing He wants to tell you is to take notice of what He made. Why? Because He loves you. Because He's a great God. Trust your ability to perceive and recognize beauty and draw conclusions therein. It's one of the ways that God can communicate with you.

DON'T DISCOUNT HIS VOICE

How many times have you sensed a voice telling you to do something but you considered it a distraction? Other times you may have felt the inkling to do something, but brushed it off as silly or too elemental to be the voice of God.

Sometimes that "distracting voice" is God trying to tell you what to do. It's His whisper. But we must be sensitive to recognize it. When we clear out the noise, confess what's on our heart, come before Him, and consider everything around us, we will be cultivating a heart to hear, a heart that is sensitive to His voice. As you train your heart to hear Him, you may find that the distracting voice is really a directing voice from the mouth of God.

How can we tell if that "distracting thought" is from God or not? Ask yourself some fundamental questions:

- Does the thought have *anything* to do with what I've been praying about?
- Does it sound more like human reasoning or spiritual direction?
- Is it consistent with the nature of God?
- Does this thought strengthen me spiritually?
- Does this thought prevent me from pursuing God's ways?

Some women sit down to read their Bibles and have a myriad of distracting thoughts: *I should do the dishes first. I've got to remember to call Mom. Maybe I should put on another coat of nail polish and let it dry while I read.* It's safe to say these are clearly thoughts from our own human nature that distract us from spending time in God's Word. Other people I know have frightening thoughts they believe are from God, such as visions that they or loved ones will be injured or killed. But Second Timothy 1:7 says God doesn't give us a spirit of fear. We also know that the Spirit of God is a Comforter, not one who instills fear. Therefore, we must ask ourselves: Is this thought in the nature of God? Does it sound like something He would say?

SEASONS OF SILENCE

Earlier, I listed four things you can do to cultivate a heart that hears God. But I would be misleading you, my friend, if I implied that God will always speak as long as you follow this formula and remain by His side. There are times, in even the most dedicated believer's life, when God appears to not be speaking at all. During these quiet times, we can practice silence, learn stillness, and get nothing but more silence. But in those times, if you remain open to God and patient, you may learn even more about Him in ways that you don't recognize at first.

My friend Betsy experienced a season of silence in which it appeared that God was not speaking to her at all. And although she never wants to return to that time in her life when things seemed very dark and quiet, she realizes now that it was a precious time through which God revealed Himself to her in a way that He never had before.

Betsy had been involved in ministry for as long as she could remember. She and her husband met through a college ministry and after marrying, served faithfully on several church staffs. Betsy's ministry was that of music and leading worship, and the desire of her heart was to know God—in all His fullness, in all His glory, in all His sufferings—so she could help usher people into God's presence through worship. Betsy remembers singing with her worship team during a practice one evening and feeling absolutely enveloped in God's presence to the point that she felt no fear.

Wow, I wish I could feel this way all the time, she remembers thinking.

Little did she know that God was wrapping her up tight for some dark days to come. The following morning, Betsy was advised by her doctor during a routine medical exam to have another mammogram. After following his orders, she was soon diagnosed with an aggressive form of breast cancer. She was told she had very little time left to live. She immediately went to God for answers, and she heard only silence. She sought direction from God's Word, but it appeared dry. She battled fear and depression as she thought about her three young children growing up without a mother.

Long days of silence passed into agonizing weeks and then months that Betsy was without any kind of word or direction from God. Betsy pored over the Scriptures and prayed till she cried, yet she still could not find the answer to her question about why all this was happening. She knew God was there, but couldn't understand why she wasn't getting answers. During that time, Betsy also was diagnosed with clinical depression and she felt herself sinking deeper and deeper down, without hope.

Betsy underwent a radical medical procedure and it, miraculously, resulted in complete eradication of the cancer. God had healed, she was sure. But He still wasn't speaking directly to her! It wasn't until about six months later, when she was walking on a path through a redwood forest, that a long-awaited voice from heaven finally spoke to her heart.

As she passed underneath a huge statuesque redwood, she noticed it suddenly became dark all around her. She looked straight up and, seeing the huge canopy of limbs and leaves over her, realized she had walked into the shade from that hovering tree. Suddenly she remembered Psalm 91: "He who dwells in the shelter of the Most High will abide in the shadow of the Almighty."

It was then that the Lord spoke to her heart: *The darkness was My hovering presence over you.*

Betsy had been dwelling in God's presence during her health crisis and pain, and had abided in His shadow. The stark realization that her darkness was because of the huge canopy of protection her Heavenly Father had placed over her, made her recall the many blessings God *had* provided her with during her time of silence. She felt the Lord's whisper on her heart: *I knew you couldn't hear My voice audibly, so I sent people to you whom you could hear. I knew you couldn't feel My presence physically, so I sent people whose hugs you could feel.*

Betsy had been seeking God's voice in a particular way, but hadn't heard it. But she *had* heard comfort and encouragement and healing from other people God had put in her path. It was Betsy's perception (just like Asaph's) that God had been silent toward her. But that hadn't been the case at all. As Betsy slowly walked out from under that hovering tree and into the sunlight again, she emerged from her perception of that dark season of silence and into the light of hearing God's voice...ever-present, ever-ringing, ever-since. Today, Betsy knows God in a way few people ever will because she had clung to Him in the darkest of circumstances and learned to trust the promise of His presence even when she didn't sense it. (And if you remember, she's the same Betsy I mentioned in chapter 4 who radiated such a presence of God and spiritual beauty because of her joy in the Lord. Now, of course, I know why.)

Even in seasons of silence when we perceive that we cannot hear God's voice, God may let us know His comforting presence in other ways so we know we are not alone. What a great communicator God is! He knows when His silence will translate to us something more meaningful than words.

START LISTENING

No matter where you are in life, the Lord wants to communicate with you. If you aren't in the habit of listening for His voice, He wants to show you how. If you've been confused about direction for your life, He wants to clarify things for you. If you simply want to know Him more, He wants to teach you all you need to know in a relationship with Him. This Heavenly Husband of yours also longs to encourage you in your need, comfort you with His promises, and affirm to You His love. But you need to cultivate a heart that listens so that you can receive what He has to say.

Spend some time in solitude and stillness, listening for the gentle words He wants to say to you. It may be nothing dramatic or sensational. It might just be something quiet and precious. But it's for you and you alone.

Hush now. Can you hear Him? Can you make out His whisper? What is it He's been waiting to say to *you*?

Preparing to Hear His Voice

Isn't it about time you and your Heavenly Husband got away together for some time alone? Here are some practical ways to practice silence and solitude before the Lord so you can hear His loving voice. Remember, sometimes He wants to give you direction, sometimes conviction, sometimes warning. But most of the time, He wants to give you gentle assurance that you are His beloved. Take a few of these steps of preparation and see if He isn't calling you His beloved as well.

1. Read Isaiah 43:7, Isaiah 55, and Psalm 103. Put your name in each passage. Then close your eyes and imagine God is saying these things directly to you. What is your response? Tell Him now. And then thank Him for His loving words.

2. Is there something God has been laying on your heart and mind lately that you've been passing off as a "distracting voice"? Ask God to clarify it to you and confirm it through Scripture or counsel from a wise, trusted Christian friend.

3. Try to arrange for 15-20 minutes alone this week to cut the noise, confess what's on your heart, clear your mind, and consider Him. Arrange the place and time, as an appointment with God. During that time, He may say something to you or He may not, but either way you are being still before Him.

4. Investigate the possibilities of attending a prayer and reflection retreat in your area. (In the state of California, call the Network of Evangelical Women in Ministry at 714-964-7236 and inquire about "The Springs.") Or plan one yourself. It could be overnight at a hotel across town in which you plan to have no contact with anyone—no television, no phone, just room service. It could be a weekend of solitude away at a cabin, desert house, or mountain resort.

Part III

Going the Distance

You've come a long way, my friend. You've seen how the Lord is the Only One who satisfies and how He loves you unconditionally, will never leave you, and sees you as beautiful in His eyes. You've grown in your relationship with Him as you've learned to approach Him with confidence, make Him your best friend, please Him, and listen to His loving voice. By now I'm sure you realize He is unlike any other and you intend to go the distance with Him.

You are about to discover what you will experience as you abide at His side and remain faithfully within His embrace. Stay with me through these last few chapters as you discover a new family, a new fulfillment, and a new future that awaits you in His arms.

10
Discovering a New Lineage

Sonja remembers feeling nothing the day her mother died. The ache and worry and unwillingness to believe her mother might die as a result of the horrible car crash days earlier left Sonja emotionally drained by the time her mother finally slipped away in the intensive care unit of the hospital. All Sonja thought about was that—at 17 years old—she, her father, and her three young brothers were suddenly left to fend for themselves.

Sonja wasn't ready for the responsibility of being her brothers' mother. And her father's caretaker. And the one to hold the family together. She couldn't help but feel that the hedge of protection that her spiritually conscious mother had built around her and the family had been removed. The next few years after her mother's death got increasingly more difficult for Sonja. Her father, who was never one to show his emotions, withdrew deeper and deeper into himself. And his inability to deal with his wife's death, his emotional distance, and his bitterness at the circumstances that had occurred, created in Sonja an insecurity about herself and the life ahead of her. In the past she had run to her mother to keep peace in the family and to make things right. But now that her mom was gone, she was left alone to sink deeper into despair.

As Sonja attempted to replace what was missing in her home, she soon felt she wasn't ready for that responsibility and she wanted nothing more than to leave home and find a life—and a family—elsewhere.

After graduating from high school, Sonja went to work at a Christian conference center, longing for a "Christian environment" that she hadn't felt in her home since her mother died. While working at the conference center, Sonja met Dave, a Christian man, and they married shortly after. Through her marriage to a godly man and through her own study of the Scriptures, Sonja began to sense a greater appreciation of God's love for her and she began to see that her problems lay not in the circumstances of her life—her mother's untimely death and her father's inability to cope with it—but in the absence of a relationship with the Lover of her soul. She needed God— in a much more intimate way than she had known Him. And she came to realize that God stood ready to meet her needs. But first she had to give up control of her life. Realizing she had nothing to lose and everything to gain, Sonja surrendered her will, her future, her entire self to the God who loved her.

As Sonja grew in her relationship with the Lord, the Spirit of God began to deliver her from her insecurities and transform her into a new woman. As this occurred, Sonja soon realized that the Lord was all she needed. Ever since her mother's death, Sonja had believed she needed a mother figure, but the Lord began to be her "mother" through His comfort and encouragement to her.[1] The Lord also "mothered her" through the ministry of the women in her church, who lived godly examples before her and showed her through their lives what it meant to walk with God.

As Sonja saw the Lord faithfully meet her every emotional need, the truth of Psalm 62:1 became a focal point for her: *My soul waits in silence for God only.* She began to depend on *God only* and she vowed to look to Him for the love she had sought for so long from her family.

A couple years into her marriage, Sonja hit a crisis point with her father and he temporarily disowned her. Because she was focused on *God only* as her Father, she had the strength and peace she needed to persevere through that dark time. During the remainder of the time that she and her father were estranged, Sonja sought comfort and peace in her Heavenly Father and, on many occasions, cried out to her "Abba"—her Daddy in heaven. She had never known a father she could call "Daddy," and now she did.

Sonja gained a family through the believers in her church, who became her brothers and sisters in the Lord. And it was through them that she discovered the love and restoration that is meant to exist in a family.

Today, Sonja is a stable and mature young woman, full of the joy of the Lord. She is secure in her relationship with her Abba Daddy, and from that stems a security in all other aspects of her life. She and Dave have been married 11 years and have three children whom they are training and instructing in the ways of the Lord. Sonja and her dad (she now refers to him as her dad, rather than just her father) have reconciled and she knows no bitterness, only gratitude for the love that her Heavenly Father gave her and the lesson she was able to learn through a fractured family. Sonja's heritage, which once looked hopeless, is a bright and beautiful one. She's a daughter of the King, a bride of the Prince, a woman much loved. And she has a family— in the Lord Jesus Christ, and in her own home with her husband and children—that she's always wanted.

PAIN IN OUR PAST

We all long for family, a sense of belonging, a feeling of healing with those whom we love. If you were blessed to be born and raised in a stable family unit, praise the Lord for that. He graciously gave you a glimpse of what a family with Him is like. But if you are like me or Sonja or countless other women and grew up with pain, neglect, or abuse, I imagine there are some longings that in many ways still seem unfulfilled.

When you have an intimate relationship with God, one that will go the distance, you can find fulfillment of that longing for family. No matter what your background, no matter what you may have inherited or experienced (certain personality traits, unfortunate situations, destructive behaviors, or sins), there is hope. In Christ, you are not only a new creation (as we saw in chapters 2 and 4), but you have a new lineage as well. A new sense of family. A fresh, new start.

FAMILY TIES

As a college student, I remained in an unhealthy relationship with a young man because I was addicted to the love in his family. His parents were the Ozzie-and-Harriet type. I couldn't imagine growing up with "Father Knows Best" and Betty Crocker, who loved to be in the kitchen and serve her family, but Dennis' parents were like that. They were involved in their church, seemed to enjoy life, and genuinely loved each other. Somehow I felt old wounds begin to heal when I was around them. And in their home, I felt a sense of security, an outpouring of love. I remember feeling that if I could just marry into this family, I could finally get what had been missing in my own home as I grew up.

Like Sonja, however, I eventually discovered I had a spiritual heritage. I had a family in the Lord. I had a Father who knows best that I could turn to any time in the pages of His Word, and I had mature brothers and sisters in the Faith who could comfort me and help me with the same sacrificial love Christ showed.

What about you? What kind of family did you come from and how has it left its marks on you? Do you find yourself trying to create in your own home the family you never had? Did you feel the effects of an absentee father, of a disinterested or distant mother? Of pain or emotional, physical, or sexual abuse? If so, you are in the company of other women who, like Sonja, have survived the scars and lived to tell of the love and grace of God which brought them out of all that and into a new spiritual heritage.

One of the women who survived the scars of a painful past was Ruth of the Bible. She left her own parents and family seeking to find a new start with the man she loved. But when he died, along with his brother and father, she was left with a choice—to go back home or find a new family. Ruth must have felt that longing for belonging, that need for a family, a desire for someone to love her and take care of her. And that longing set her on an incredible journey that would lead her to True Love.

Ruth's Story

Ruth grew up in the land of Moab, a country of godless people. So it's safe to assume there were a lot of problems back at home when she married one of Naomi's sons, a man from Judah. But her new husband died shortly after and so did his brother, who legally would have been the one to marry Ruth and take care of her after his brother's death. Ruth's husband, brother-in-law, and father-in-law were all dead, leaving just Ruth, her mother-in-law Naomi, and her sister-in-law Orpah. How quickly the family had disintegrated! And they had no one to provide for them. So Naomi and the two young widows headed back to Naomi's homeland.

On the way to Judah, Naomi urged her daughters-in-law to go back home to their parents' families. Orpah conceded. But for some reason, Ruth didn't want to return home.

We don't know why Ruth didn't go back to her family. It's possible she felt more love from her Jewish mother-in-law than she did among her entire family back in Moab. Whether it was her childhood home that haunted her, or her love for Naomi that compelled her, Ruth decided against going back home and continued on toward Judah. These two women, without a soul to care for them, hoped to find one of Naomi's old relatives to take them in. So they pressed on to a place where they might find some sense of family.

When they arrived in Bethlehem, it was Ruth's integrity in staying with her mother-in-law and trusting that God would provide for them that attracted her to a man named Boaz, who was a relative. And by God's provision, Boaz became Ruth's "kinsman redeemer"—a term used for a relative who had legal right to marry a woman and give her an inheritance.[2] Boaz was a kind, gentle, and loving man, and he redeemed Ruth (by marrying her) out of his love for her, not his obligation. Boaz became Ruth's provider, sustainer, and lover. And Boaz gave Ruth a family as well. Through God's grace, this pagan woman with a painful past became the great-grandmother of King David and an ancestress of Jesus of Nazareth, who was born from David's line hundreds of years later.[3] In looking for love and a sense of family, Ruth found a husband, an inheritance, and a spiritual lineage she had never dreamed of.

Like Ruth, you and I have a "Kinsman Redeemer" as well. He's the One who takes us as His own—not out of obligation, but out of His love for us—and in His kind and gentle nature loves us, provides for us, and gives us a new family. In the Lord we find, like Ruth found in Boaz, a Provider, a Sustainer, a Lover. And we end up with a spiritual heritage like we never dreamed. Unlike Boaz, however, our Redeemer will never die. And the inheritance He gives us will go beyond the grave and into eternity with us. Through our new spiritual lineage in the Lord, we have become royalty, daughters of the King, brides of the Prince of Peace.

YOUR SPIRITUAL INHERITANCE

What happened to Ruth can happen to you, too...in fact, if you are a Christian, it already did. You married your Kinsman Redeemer back when you gave your life to Him as the Only One who satisfies. Your lineage—your children, the heritage you build in your home, the legacy of your life—is a blessed one. And like Ruth, perhaps you will be known as the woman who left everything else behind (including a painful past and splintered family) and followed the Lord God.

When we talk of inheritance, we speak of the things that we are entitled to, the things we have coming. Here on earth it may include your parents' house, some savings and stocks, perhaps some property. Whatever it includes, and whatever the net value here on earth, it won't go past this earth and with you into eternity. But what you are entitled to because of your family ties with God is eternal. It will stand the test of time and accompany you into the realms of eternity.

Just what does this spiritual inheritance include?

Adoption into God's family

The Bible says we have received in Christ "a spirit of adoption as sons."[4] There is a common misconception *all* people are God's children because He created everyone.

We are all God's *creation*, but we are not all God's children. Formerly, you and I belonged to this earth and the
ruler of this earth (Satan), until God graciously adopted
us into His family. When He gave us this "sonship," we
became His child.[5]

An inheritance in heaven

When we become God's children, we inherit the right
to all that is ours in Christ. Romans 8:17 says that Jesus
redeemed us so that we might "receive...the Spirit of sonship" (NIV). That means we have a right to everything that
the *real* Son, Jesus, has (except godhood, of course).
Because we are joint heirs with Jesus, we can have the
eternal life that He has, the home in heaven that He has,
the ear of the Father like He has, and the riches untold
that He has in heaven. We have, as our inheritance:

- eternal life without pain, sorrow or tears
- new immortal bodies that won't grow old or wear
  down
- perfection of holiness so we no longer sin
- crowns for our work here on earth (that we will
  gladly lay down at Jesus' feet)[6]

These are just some of the imperishable rewards that
we will receive in heaven. But we have access to some of
our inheritance now while we're still here on earth.
Philippians 4:19 says that God will supply all our needs
according to "His riches in glory in Christ Jesus." Those
riches are available to us when we are in need, just for the
asking. Now *that* is an inheritance!

Another aspect of our heavenly inheritance is that we
are heirs of God's kingdom. That makes you and me
daughters of the King and able to share in the privileges
that accompany that. We don't have to live like palace

slaves; we are royalty when it comes to our position in Christ. Galatians 4:7 says we are "no longer a slave, but a son; and if a son, then an heir through God."

The privilege of calling Him "Daddy"

Scripture doesn't just say we can call God our Father or our Dad. The Bible tells us we have been given the right, through our adoption, to call Him "Daddy." (In Romans 8:15, the English word that is most close in meaning to the Aramaic word "Abba" is *Papa* or *Daddy*.)

Jesus used this affectionate, loving term for the Father when He prayed "Abba!" in the Garden of Gethsemane shortly before He was arrested and crucified. In crying out "Abba!" Jesus showed His dependence on Daddy while contemplating His impending death.[7] We can call upon our Heavenly Daddy as personally as God's own loving Son, Jesus, did. Now that is a privilege! That is affection. And that is love between a Daddy and daughter.

My earliest recollections of time with my Daddy are when he would take me for rides on his bicycle across town to Fred's Café when I was three or four years old. Every afternoon, Dad would get out his bike and I would jump at the opportunity to sit in front of him on his bike with just his arm around me as he pedaled across town, over the railroad tracks, and into the dirt parking lot of Fred's. Even though it was a long ride, neither of us wore a helmet, the bike had no handbrakes (and many times Dad rode without hands), and we had to cross those bumpy railroad tracks every time, I never for a moment feared that I would fall or be hurt. I was up close next to Daddy. Daddy was holding me. Daddy would keep me safe.

It's often been said that daughters have a special place in the hearts of their daddies. It's no different with our

Daddy in heaven. Every child of God has a special place in His heart. He asks us to ride with Him and He holds us close where we'll be safe, even over the bumpy railroad tracks of life.

Did you have a relationship with your father in which you could freely call him "Daddy"? If so, that is a blessing...God was giving you a glimpse of the love and affection He has for you. If not, this too is a blessing because God is giving you an opportunity now to call Him Daddy and experience the closeness you never had with your earthly father.

A new heritage

Psalm 16 says that we who are God's children have a new heritage, meaning a new family history and a new family line. When you became a child of God, you became a descendant of the great people in God's family, like Abraham, Jacob, Joseph, Moses, and so on.

Whenever I hear someone who is a member of God's family complain about their relatives or inheritance here on earth, I like to show them the beautiful truths about our new family in Psalm 16. In fact, I first discovered this when I was writing to Sonja, about her family troubles years ago:

> • **The Lord is the portion of my inheritance and my cup (verse 5a)**
>
> If I don't have anything to inherit here on earth, that's okay. I may not have a portion in lands or houses or stocks or bonds, but I have a portion in the Lord and His inheritance. I have a portion in salvation and that is more than enough. Like the old hymn says: "I'd rather have Jesus than silver or gold...."

- **Thou dost support my lot (verse 5b)**

     If I feel I don't have any support spiritually or otherwise from my earthly family, that's okay. The Lord is the one who supports me and encourages me. *If God is for us, who can be against us?*[8]

- **The lines have fallen to me in pleasant places (verse 6a)**

     Despite the unpleasantness we may have dealt with in our families, just the fact that we know God is evidence of His grace. Because He drew us out of our situation and into the warm embrace of His family, He has preserved our "line" and put us in a pleasant place.

- **Indeed, my heritage is beautiful to me (verse 6b)**

     Because we are numbered with the sons of God, including all those pillars of faith listed in Hebrews 11, we have a beautiful heritage. And the grace of God that set us apart for His glory cannot be compared in value or importance to *any* earthly heritage.

TIGHTENING THE TIES THAT BIND

So what will you do with this newfound appreciation for the family you have in Christ Jesus? In chapter 7, I gave you a three-point plan for pleasing God based on Philippians 3:13-14. Because the principles of forgetting, focusing, and forging ahead are so applicable to many aspects of our lives, I have another three-point plan, based on those same verses, for starting a new spiritual heritage.

1. *Forget what lies behind*—particularly the pain of the past. Lay it before God and repent of the bitterness you may be holding onto and forgive others in your family for the hurts you may have suffered on account of them.

2. *Look forward to what lies ahead*—in the family you now have. Invest in your spiritual family by serving the members of the family of God and by seeking heavenly rather than earthly riches and rewards.

3. *Press on*—by creating a new spiritual lineage for your family. Be a family that loves and serves God with all you have—time, money, and resources. Impress upon your children the inheritance they have waiting in heaven and the characteristics and lessons they are learning in this life that will last into eternity. If you are single, live in the majesty of a daughter of the King, helping other royal sons and daughters to discover the beauty of their spiritual heritage as well.

PUTTING IT TO THE TEST

My friend Christi is an example of a young woman who applied these principles to her life in the wake of losing her father at nine years old (to an infection) and her husband at 26 (to an affair and painful divorce). Instead of focusing on the loss of the major men in her life, she put the pain of the past behind her, looked forward to the fact that the Lord is her Father and her Husband, and pressed on. Although Christi's mother never remarried, and Christi, herself, is still single, she has moved forward in her life by adopting an orphan from China who had no father or mother. Today, Christi continues to press on not only by being a mother to a motherless and fatherless child, but by instructing Paige, her little one, in the ways of the Lord and creating a spiritual legacy to pass on to her new daughter and her daughter's family after her. Although a series of events made things difficult in Christi's childhood home and newly married home, she has not let it affect Paige's home.

LOVING YOUR NEW LINEAGE

When it comes to family, do you think first of what you have in the Lord Jesus Christ? If there's still pain in your past, see it as an avenue and doorway to a greater sense of love from your Heavenly Father. Let Him marvelously make up for what you didn't have in a family here on earth.

Today Sonja readily praises God over what He divinely allowed to happen in her home because she realizes that through her loss, she learned of a greater love. In a recent letter to me she wrote, "Had I not known devastation through the loss of my mother, had I not wept many tears over the lack of a meaningful and loving relationship with my father, I would not have received help in my time of need and I doubt that I would ever have come to the higher ground I was led to through those things."

Sonja, in going the distance with her True Love, has discovered that the Lord is enough. She is realizing the joy of contentment with *God only*. And she is continuing to experience the Lord Jesus Christ and her fellow believers in Christ as members of a wonderful and caring family.

Won't you let the Lord Jesus Christ and your brothers and sisters in the Lord make up for what may have been lacking in *your* family?

Focusing on a New Family

We can't fully experience the joy of our new lineage if we're still living in the baggage of our old one. Work through these exercises as a way of forgetting what's in the past, focusing on what lies ahead, and moving forward with your new family in the Lord. It will make your intimacy with Him all the more meaningful as you make His family a part of your life together:

1. If you grew up watching "The Waltons," "The Brady Bunch," or "The Cosby Show," your perception of what a family should be like may be a little idealized. Bring to the Lord the disappointments and problems you faced in your own family and ask Him to help you release any expectations, bitterness, or resentments. Then, ask Him to help you focus on what you have in your spiritual family instead.

2. Read Psalm 16 aloud.
- How has God *supported your lot* during your growing-up and adult years?
- How have the lines *fallen to you in pleasant places*, despite any pain that may have existed?
- In what ways do you consider your spiritual heritage *beautiful*?

3. If you received a good solid spiritual foundation from a parent, grandparent, or another relative, write a letter expressing your gratitude to that person. Let him or her know his or her investment was worth it. Just writing the letter may bring some blessings to mind that you had long since forgotten.

4. What will you do this week to begin shaping your own family's spiritual heritage? Share your plan with a friend or pastor who could encourage you and hold you accountable.

11

Living with a New Purpose

At 58, Jane had nearly given up on life.

Her body was worn out from years of drug abuse. Her heart was hardened by a life of sin. And she was tired of running—from the law, from herself, from God. She had nothing—and no one—to live for. Her husband was dead. Her son was in jail. And her daughter hadn't spoken to her in years. Jane was literally homeless, helpless, and hopeless.

Jane wandered into the doors of a little church one Sunday morning as a last resort. *Just maybe I can find some help,* she thought. She shared her story with a couple she sat next to during the church service. The couple had compassion on Jane and, within a week, found her a live-in job caring for an elderly gentleman. The couple began driving Jane to church each week, and as this weary shell-of-a-woman began to gain knowledge of who she was in the sight of God, and what her life meant to Him, she began to gain a sense of hope. Little by little, Jane's physical needs—for food, shelter, an income, and eventually, even a car—were met through her simple, child-like trust in God. Jane was amazed at how her life began to fall in place when she trusted this God she hadn't known before.

After a year of seeing how God had cared for her, how He had provided for all her needs through the church she was attending, and how He had suffered on a cross for her sin so she could live with Him eternally, Jane fell to her knees in repentance of her old life and in commitment to her One True Love. When she got back up on her feet, she realized she not only had a new life, she had a new purpose as well.

Today, at 61, Jane is full of the energy and vibrancy of a 30-year-old. She loves her home, her job, her church, and her Lord. She works in a home caring for and ministering to elderly women where she's referred to as "the angel." She has reconciled with her children and seen the Lord work in their lives as well. She serves faithfully in the little church where she found hope, and she has become a beam of light to those around her as she constantly gives God the credit for where she is today. Jane is considered one of the most compassionate women in her church, extending mercy to those who are now helpless and hopeless like she once was.

Jane found a new life with her Heavenly Husband. And with that life came a new purpose, a new hope, and a new reason to live. Jane now realizes that her prior attempts to end her life failed because God had a purpose for her. And not only is her *life* worth living, but *everything* she does has meaning when she does it for the One who gave Himself for her. She is still here on this earth for the wonderful privilege of bringing glory to God, through a transformed life, a powerful testimony, and a heart to worship Him. Jane is no longer one of life's throwaways. She is an asset in the kingdom of God.

SEARCHING FOR PURPOSE

All of us, at one time or another, struggle with questions like "What's my purpose?" and, "What should I be doing with my life?" Perhaps we've never sunk to the depths of despair as Jane did, but undoubtedly we often wonder what our purpose in life is all about.

What is *your* purpose as the bride of Christ? Why did He extend His loving arm to *you* and bring you out of the ordinary life you knew and into an extraordinary one of close relationship with Him?

Just like with Jane, God wants to get the glory for what He's been able to do in your life. You don't have to have a powerful, earth-shaking testimony like Jane's to draw people to the Lord. All you have to have is the joy that comes from a close, intimate relationship with Him. That gives the Lord all He needs to work with to help you experience your new purpose here on earth. He wants your friends and family and neighbors and co-workers to stop and take notice of what has happened in you to make you so secure, so full of joy, so "with it" like a woman much loved. This purpose He has for you is simply to live in the love He has given you so that others see you as a testimony of what God can do. And as you do this, you'll enjoy life more abundantly and experience intimacy like you never knew it. And Your Heavenly Husband will be pleased that you are living out your purpose.

When I married my husband, I went from independent career woman to wife. Suddenly my purpose shifted from a person who looks after myself to one who looks after my husband, supports him, encourages him, works alongside him to accomplish certain goals, and shares my life and heart with him. The one thing that changed the most concerning my purpose in life is that I became a team with my husband. I was no longer an individual living a separate and independent life.

When you committed yourself to the Lord, your True Love, you went from independent woman to wife as well. Suddenly your purpose shifted from a person who looks after herself to one who looks to her True Love, supporting Him (in proclaiming to others your love for Him), encouraging Him (by your commitment to Him), working alongside Him to accomplish certain goals, and sharing your life and heart with Him. You became a team with your Heavenly Husband, and should no longer continue to live a separate and independent life.

CHASING AFTER WIND

Every woman has needs for purpose and significance. I know of several women—Christian women—who have tried all sorts of things, looking for their purpose in life. They have sold cosmetics one month, represented another company the next. Then they were in and out of classes at a community college, toying with the idea of getting an education. Then they were considering foster parenting, hosting international students in their home, starting their own business, or having another baby. This endless pursuit, a sort of chasing after wind, is driven by the idea that we will eventually find something that will make us feel significant, fulfilled, or (if we're not bringing home our own paycheck) productive. But the search for fulfillment, apart from our relationship with God, will leave us empty and searching for more.

In chapter 1 I spoke of the dried-out bush (in Jeremiah 17) that we become like when we look to people or relationships for our fulfillment. The same thing happens when we look to a job, career, position, title, or hobby as the key to fulfillment in our lives. We will live like "stony wastes in the wilderness," dry and unproductive.[1] Instead, God wants us to be one who looks to Him (and our life in Him) for our purpose and fulfillment. Then we will be like that tree planted by streams of water, always refreshed, always growing, blooming to our potential and bearing much fruit.[2]

As women of God we never have to live like dried-out, barren bushes in the desert, seeking purpose and fulfillment in our lives. We know our purpose (which happens to be our key to fulfillment as well), and it's spelled out in black and white in God's Word.

YOUR PURPOSE—TO GLORIFY GOD

God makes it very clear what He expects of us in our relationship with Him: to glorify Him in all we do. To glorify Him with all we have. To glorify Him with who we are. That is our purpose. And we can find ours in Him.

There are many ways to glorify God and fulfill our purpose. We glorify God by:

Doing it all for Him

First Corinthians 10:31 tells us to do *all things* for the glory of God. What does that mean? It means washing the dishes, folding the laundry, and cleaning the house to the best of our ability for God alone. You can mother your child to the glory of God, serve your husband to the glory of God, love your neighbor to the glory of God, and so on. You can complete and present a project at work to the glory of God, or set a standard of integrity so others see you and marvel at the work of God in you. Or you can simply live a life of newness in Him, like Jane, and have others stand back and say, "Wow...what made the change in *her*?" Doing everything for God's glory means He is the One who gets the credit for the fine job you did. When others see that your work was not something you alone could have done, but something that God enabled you to do or something you did out of love and obedience to Him, then God gets the praise and the glory.

Performing good works

Ephesians 2:10 says we were created to accomplish certain good works that God had already planned for us before we were born. Talk about purpose in life! Talk about a destiny! And when others see us accomplish those assigned works, which we could do only through God's anointing, they glorify our Father in heaven.[3]

Using our talents and abilities for Him

Every one of us can do some things—or at least one thing—exceptionally well. Doing those things in a way that brings glory to God is fulfilling His purpose for us. If you're musically talented, you could bring glory to God by singing in your church's choir or on its worship team. If you're a whiz at accounting, you could glorify God by helping your church with its financial records. If you're wonderful with children, glorifying God could mean reaching out to the little ones in your neighborhood. And if you have a natural knack for decorating, bringing glory to the Lord could mean adding your touch to the women's spring luncheons or creating and supporting themes for your church's fellowship potlucks.

Exercising our spiritual gifts

First Corinthians 12:7 says we all have been given at least one spiritual gift by the Lord. That means we each have the ability to do something that we absolutely cannot do apart from Him. Whether our gift is teaching the Word of God, encouraging others to live a godly life, administrating certain ministries, or helping and serving, using that gift to build up God's body (your local church) or encourage others in their walk with God is fulfilling your purpose. (The gifts of the Spirit are listed in 1 Corinthians 12:7-11, 28 and Romans 12:6-8.)

Living a holy and blameless life before Him

Romans 12:1-2 says that it is God's will for each of us to not be conformed to this world and its ways, but to be transformed to the Lord's ways with a new mind. It is also God's purpose for us to give our entire bodies to Him so He can be glorified in our holy habits and healthy lives.

Becoming molded to the image of Christ

Romans 8:28-29 says that God causes all things in our life to work together for our good *so* that we can become more like Christ. When we become more and more like our True Love, reflecting His character, His heart, and His actions, we are fulfilling His purpose for us. We are pleasing God.

Increasing in the knowledge of God

God wants us to know His will, His Word, and how to walk in a way that pleases Him (Colossians 1:9-10). He wants us to study His Word to the point where we can live it with our eyes shut, teach it to others, and counsel with it. God's purpose for us is that we grow and mature in His Word and be able to defend its truths against anyone who challenges them[4] (2 Timothy 2:15, KJV preferred). Think about that purpose for a moment: to know God and His Word as much as we possibly can before we go to live with Him for all eternity. That is why discovering our purpose is essential in going the distance with Him.

YOUR PURPOSE—TO MINISTER ON GOD'S BEHALF

As you go the distance with your True Love, you will eventually want to serve Him in a more fulfilling and meaningful way. Every woman I've ever met who is truly intimate with God is involved in some aspect of ministry—ministering to others in her home, neighborhood, church, or workplace.

When I began serving on the executive committee of a Christian women's organization, I was surprised at the great commitment expressed by the other women in the group. But as I got to know each one, it made sense to me that they were involved with this organization: As they developed a heart for God, He took them further in their pursuit of ways to serve Him and minister to the hearts of others.

A woman who loves God will serve Him. That doesn't necessarily mean serving Him in the spotlight in a leading or teaching ministry. Sometimes it means serving Him behind the scenes, being willing to go where He calls, do what He asks, and be what He wants us to be out of sheer love for Him. Some women never plan for a high-profile ministry, but if that's where God can use them, He will develop their heart and their spiritual gifts and gently push them out into the public. Others, He molds and shapes by having them influence lives one-on-one, in the privacy of a home or the comfort of a coffee shop. However God chooses for us to serve Him, a woman who loves God with all her heart will follow His call wherever it leads, even if it's to places she had never planned.

Extending beyond the job

All during my growing-up years I loved to write. So in high school I determined I would major in journalism and write for a living.

Shortly after graduating from college, I married Hugh and worked for four years writing for a chain of newspapers in Southern California while Hugh finished Bible school. But as I grew in my loveship with the Lord, He began to place on my heart a desire to write for women as a ministry rather than write for the world as a job. On occasion I took an opportunity at the newspaper to write a "viewpoint" or editorial. And soon I realized my passion was to soothe breaking hearts rather than cover breaking news. My interest wasn't in writing stories on transportation issues in crowded, commuter-crazy Southern California, but in writing words that would convict hearts that had crowded God out of their lives. By the time I left the newsroom to have a baby, I knew I would never write in the same capacity again. My writing career from that point forward would focus on encouraging women in their walk with the Lord.

During the next five years of my life, I stayed home with my daughter and began to write Bible studies for my women's group at church and Bible class curricula for adults. I also spent my time writing letters of encouragement to women and counseling and instructing them, one on one, in God's Word. From that time of redirecting my passion into a ministry, the chapters of this book developed.

In taking me deeper with Himself, God created in me the desire to live for Him in a more intense way, to write for Him and to use all that I had in a way that served Him. As our devotion to serving Him becomes a bigger part of our lives, it eventually becomes our whole life.

Now, I realize not every woman is in a position to give up her paying job to pursue her passion. I was fortunate that my husband was willing to make the financial sacrifice for me to give up my paycheck (and health insurance and retirement benefits) to redirect my career so I could serve the Lord. Granted, it paid little (more like nothing!) financially, but I found fulfillment in living out God's purpose for me. And God has been faithful in turning my passion and service into a ministry that has begun to meet our financial needs as well.

Maybe that's not an option for you. Maybe your marketable skills don't appear to lend themselves to a spiritual slant. But whether you're a business executive, a waitress, a schoolteacher, a child-care provider, or a stay-at-home mom, you can turn what you do into a ministry by refocusing why you do it and who you do it for. Nearly anything can become a ministry through which God is glorified. We just need to pray for a way.

Praying for a way

Pam is a 50-year-old bailiff for a county court house. Her job is to keep order in a courtroom. That, in itself, doesn't appear to be a job she can turn into a ministry. After all, she can't share her testimony on the county's time clock, or become one who propagates her faith to people she comes in contact with. But as Pam began developing intimacy with God, she began praying for a way to serve Him and fulfill her purpose as a woman of God within the job she already had.

As Pam started praying for opportunities, God started sending them her way. Pam began to gently touch the shoulders of anguished wives who watched their hand-cuffed husbands be led away from the courtroom. She began to put her arms around frightened children who became wards of the court. She talked compassionately with distraught families of rape and murder victims. And she started offering to hurting individuals four of the most encouraging words some of them will ever hear: *I'll pray for you.* There is no shortage of pain in Pam's line of work. So there are no shortages of opportunities for ministry. Pam's heart for the Lord pushes her to go beyond her job and see her purpose in life: to serve God through ministry right where she is in life.

Praying for words

Janice supervises the food service at her community's high school. Food service doesn't appear to be a ministry.

Yet Janice works with many women who have problems in their lives. Because Janice loves the Lord and desires to serve Him in all that she does, she began praying for a way to serve Him within the parameters of her job. And she began praying for the words to say to the women she supervised. Sure enough, God began sending the opportunities—and the words—her way. Today Janice offers a glimpse of her Heavenly Husband to the women in her kitchen through her loving, listening ear, her godly advice from her knowledge of God's Word, and her discernment to know when someone needs a gentle rebuke and when she needs words of encouragement. Janice has a ministry not because she is *in* ministry, but because she loves God and prays for a way to extend beyond her job and fulfill her purpose.

What Now?

How can *you* live out your purpose as you go the distance with your True Love? In what ways can you extend yourself beyond your job or beyond your front door and into the hearts of hurting people around you who need to meet the God who has changed your life?

Pray for a way. Watch for opportunities. And then take them. They may start out small at first, but as you are faithful in a little, God will eventually give you more. As you pray, watch for and work through opportunities to serve God right where you are in life. And you will experience the thrill and fulfillment of discovering—and living out—your new purpose in Him.

Get Ready for the Ride

Get ready, because you are in for some exciting days ahead in living out your purpose for the glory of God.

What should you expect as you begin to look for opportunities to live out your new purpose in Him?

Sometimes God pushes you out of your comfort zone to show you the great things He has in store for you. Sometimes He gently prods you until you head in the direction where you can serve Him more and give Him greater glory. And sometimes He keeps you right where you are and gives you more opportunities than you realized were there.

If you think you've experienced a full life so far, just wait. Living it 100 percent for His glory by blurring the lines between your spiritual life and vocational life, and bringing them together in one life lived solely for the Lord, will take you to a destination you never imagined. You will not only go the distance in serving Him, but you'll enjoy the trip immensely. Hold on—you're in for the ride of your life!

Pursuing Your Purpose

Here are a few ways you can begin to discover—and live out—your new purpose in God. Remember, as you are faithful in a little, He will give you more. And as you fulfill your purpose in Him day to day, you will experience greater joy in an obedient, intimate, and purposeful life.

1. Proverbs 16:3 says, "Commit your works to the LORD and your plans will be established." What is one thing you have always dreamed of doing for the Lord? What is it that caused you to give up on that dream? Bring that dream—and those plans—to the Lord today and ask Him to reevaluate them in conjunction with your purpose. Then be open to wherever He might lead.

2. Read First Corinthians 12:7-11, 28 and Romans 12:6-8. What spiritual gift or gifts has God given you? How are you using them in your church or related ministry? As you become faithful in using those gifts, He may grant you more opportunities for fulfilling your purpose in Him.

3. What are some ways you can glorify God and show others a glimpse of your Heavenly Husband in your life right now as a...

- Friend:

- Neighbor:

- Wife:

- Mother or grandmother:

- Student:

- Employee (or employer):

- Member of your church:

- Member of a community organization:

4. Has God been gently prodding you to leave your comfort zone and go out in faith to serve Him in a more fulfilling way? If so, pray diligently about this and seek godly counsel from trusted Christian advisers. God may have a special purpose waiting for you in the days ahead!

12
Experiencing a Future Together

Lynn walked slowly up the path between the trees, her eyes shifting with uncertainty. The brisk wind whipped through her veil, blowing the curls around her face. The gold sequin on her white raw silk gown glittered as it reflected the sunlight that was beginning to set on Monterey Bay. The guests, seated on both sides of the path Lynn walked upon, rose to their feet as the bride walked past. It was a picture-perfect day. But from where I stood, next to the flower girl and the minister, I could see that Lynn was not smiling. Even on her wedding day, she was not smiling at her future.

Perhaps Lynn was thinking about all that she couldn't smile about in her life. At 34 years old, Lynn's wedding day did not come as soon as she had hoped, nor in the way she had envisioned since childhood. Her mother's quick, agonizing death from cancer left Lynn devastated a few years earlier, followed by her father's hasty remarriage and abandonment of Lynn. Confusion, anger, bitterness and depression had set in, and there were times during the past few years when it took everything Lynn had to get herself out of bed and face another day. Thoughts of ending her life—and the pain—were all too real. Many times she struggled with the feeling that she had no future. But she pressed on, believing that somewhere there had to be a future and a hope.

Now as she walked down that path, perhaps she was thinking about the pain of the past few years, of her estranged family seated in the front row, of the seat (now occupied by her father's new wife) where her mother would have sat if she had lived to see this day. She may have been thinking of the questions that would await her after the ceremony from people she hadn't spoken with in years.

As Lynn continued to make her way toward the archway, her eyes remained distant—until at last she shifted her glance to the left of me where Randy, her fiancée, stood waiting for her to reach the end of her walk. Immediately her eyes brightened, her smile appeared, and her steps became more confident. As Lynn continued to walk forward, in the presence of her wedding party and guests, she did it with a smile—not because the pain had disappeared, but because she had focused on the one who loved her and was waiting for her at the end of the path.

As Lynn and Randy joined hands, the minister read the words they had written for each other: "No longer will we feel the rain, for we will be each other's shelter. No longer will we feel the cold, for we will be each other's warmth. No longer will we experience loneliness, for we will be each other's comfort."

As the minister continued reading, I turned around to look at the sky behind me and the sea down the hill beneath me. The sun was setting on Monterey Bay and its reflection made the waves appear gold as they crashed gently against the red rocks. And peeking out from the side of a darkened cloud was the hint of a rainbow. (It had drizzled that morning as I held Lynn's hand at this exact spot on the hill and prayed for the sun to return.) As I focused on that rainbow, I remembered the faithfulness of God in holding back the rain on many occasions in my own life and His faithfulness in keeping the vows He has made to me.

Despite the various storms in my life, I have not felt the rain because *He has been my shelter.* Although the crisp wind on that cold March day made me shiver in my bare-backed dress, I remembered that so often I have not felt the cold because *He has been my warmth.* As I looked out among the guests and thought about my husband back home who was not able to make the trip with me that weekend, I remembered that I have never really been alone because *He has been my comfort.*

As the minister continued to lead Lynn and Randy through their vows, my thoughts led me back to the day I committed my life to the Lord. And I realized that since the day He took me in His arms, I have had a future worth celebrating. It's been a future of shelter, warmth, comfort, and togetherness. It's been a future of dreams, plans, and pleasures. There have been times that have appeared rough, but my life—and now my future—is not about what has happened or what will happen. Rather, it is all about Who I know and Who will continue to live the rest of my days with me.

WHAT ABOUT YOU?

When you think about *your* future, what comes to mind? Are you overwhelmed with some of the things you've been through and wondering if more such circumstances are waiting just around the corner? Are you looking at the "what ifs," the painful possibilities, the barrel full of uncertainties? Are you, like Lynn, walking hesitantly down the path without a smile on your face because you're just not sure what awaits you?

Lynn was able to smile and face her future only when she looked into the eyes of the one who loved her. Yet Lynn was marrying a man—a sinner who, despite his intended vows, would still let her down at times. There will probably be days in Lynn's life when the rain will come and her new husband will not be able to shelter her. There may be days when it gets so cold that Randy will not be able to provide the warmth Lynn needs. And there may be times when she feels so alone that her husband's comfort will not be enough.

But the One who stands waiting for you and me is different. Our Heavenly Husband is perfect[1] and absolutely incapable of letting us down. We don't just have *hope* for a great future, we have His personal promise and guarantee!

HAPPILY EVER AFTER?

In the past eleven chapters we've learned of our Heavenly Husband's love for us, learned how to love Him in return, and discovered more about our inheritance in Him and our purpose in Him. By now we should be well aware of the fact that we are headed for a wonderful future in the arms of our True Love. By now we should be convinced that we have a Prince who is waiting to whisk us away. By now we should be well into living "happily ever after."

So if that's true, where *is* the happily ever after?

If you're like me, you grew up on dreams of romance and hoping for the "happily ever after." And in your favorite fairy tales, the impoverished, mistreated woman became a princess and lived the rest of her days in a palace with a prince. But in spite of what we've been told from childhood about happiness and romance, our happily ever after is not about what we have. It's about Who we know and how well we know Him. Snow White, Sleeping Beauty, and Cinderella all faced a "happily ever after" as they headed toward the palace to be the bride of a prince they barely knew. But we have it so much better. We're headed to a mansion in heaven (as we discovered in chapter 10) and we'll live forever with the Prince we already know intimately and love wholeheartedly. It doesn't get any better than that.

Still, we tend to fear our future. We let things that we have or don't have and fears of what might or might not happen hinder us from experiencing our happily ever after with the One who stands waiting to give it to us.

FACING OUR FEARS

Sometimes money—or the lack of it—causes us to fear our future. If we didn't invest in a 401k plan at work or we don't have a nice nest egg to look forward to upon retirement, the future might look a little scary. Many women today don't know where their finances will be next month, let alone several years down the road. When we focus on our finances, our future can look scary and we can lose sight of our happily ever after.

For some women, health concerns can cloud their vision of a happily ever after. We fear when our bodies begin to wear down with age. We fear when we discover a lump that must be biopsied. We may be living with the fear that cancer will show up, spread, or return, or that arthritis or some other ailment will rob us of our joy.

Sometimes we fear our future because we don't want to be alone. Maybe the one we planned to spend the rest of our days with is no longer around or maybe the one we had hoped to marry chose someone else. Single mothers raising children without help, divorcees with no apparent hope of remarrying, widows missing the man they loved all their life long all know the fear of facing a future of loneliness.

Yet in going the distance with our True Love, we must come to terms with this: Our future is not about what we have or don't have. It's not about what might or might not happen. Our future is *all about* who we know and how well we know Him.

BACK TO THEIR FUTURE

Many women in the Bible had a promising future. But too often they focused on what they didn't have rather than on who they knew. As a result, they never experienced the happily ever after that God had intended for them.

For example, Eve, the first woman created, had a glorious future. She had no baggage in her past, no sins that haunted her, no legacies to live up to—just a fresh start as the first woman who ever lived. She had, quite literally, the perfect husband. And she lived in a perfect garden home that needed no weeding. She didn't have to work (neither did her husband) and they had no children, no sleepless nights, no bills to pay, no nasty neighbors, no annoying in-laws, and no laundry to wash (they wore no clothes, remember?). But Eve began to want something more—the mind of God—and she ended up with a future far different than what she could've had.[2]

Sarah, Abraham's wife, was getting old and was still childless. She must have felt she had no future. And when God promised to make her the mother of nations but He didn't deliver as quickly as she had hoped, she arranged to get a son another way and ended up experiencing a future that was less perfect than the one God had planned for her.[3]

Rebekah, the wife of Isaac, met her husband in a beautifully romantic way.[4] She had a promising future as a woman much loved and the mother of "two nations."[5] But after giving birth to the twins Esau and Jacob, Rebekah was more concerned about her youngest son's future than her own and she tricked and schemed against her husband to give Jacob a future God had already promised him in the first place. Rebekah didn't focus on the One who held her and her son's future in His hands.[6]

Rachel and Leah, two sisters who rivaled each other in childbearing, competed viciously with each other for their future. And they, in turn, never really experienced what God may have ultimately planned for them.[7]

In the case of every woman I've named, their future was not about what they had or didn't have. Their future, their happily ever after, was about *who* they knew. But they never really knew or trusted God in the way that we ought to.

OUR GOLDEN OPPORTUNITY

We're told in the New Testament, "No eye has seen, no ear has heard, no mind has conceived what God has prepared for those who love him *but God has revealed it to us by his Spirit*" (1 Corinthians 2:9-10 NIV, emphasis added).

That tells me that these women in the Old Testament couldn't see or hear or even conceive what it was like to know God personally through a relationship with Jesus. They knew God as their Creator, Lawgiver, and Judge. But they didn't know Him as their Savior, their Lord, their Heavenly Husband. They didn't know Jesus through the Scriptures that describe His life and record His words. And they didn't have the indwelling Holy Spirit within them to make known to them the presence of God in their lives. No wonder they didn't celebrate their future of intimacy with God. They didn't have the kind of opportunity we have for intimacy with Jesus, the Lover of our soul.

SMILING AT OUR FUTURE

Because you and I can come to know our Heavenly

Husband intimately, through a close personal relationship with Jesus, we can smile at our future despite the circumstances that may occur during our lifetime. In the midst of the uncertainties—like finances, health, and relationships—we have an absolute certainty: a future of intimacy with Jesus. And that means a future of hope.

In Jeremiah 29:11, God reassures us with these words: "For I know the plans that I have for you…plans for welfare and not for calamity to give you a future and a hope." We tend to think that this passage refers to our future in heaven. But I think that God is referring to the wonderful future we can experience on earth as well, when we know His Son intimately. You see, centuries later, Jesus in essence echoed His Father's words when He said, "I come that [you] might have life, and have it abundantly" (John 10:10). In today's language, Jesus might have said, "I have come so you can experience intimacy with Me and have a happily ever after."

WHAT KIND OF A FUTURE?

When God says He has a future for us, what does that really mean? And what is so great about this future of intimacy with Jesus?

A future of fulfillment

We've seen in the first chapter of this book how Jesus is the Only One who can satisfy. And we've seen in the most recent chapter, how we can find our purpose in Him by glorifying Him in all we do. When we look to a future of intimacy with God, we find fulfillment and we can be like the tree in Jeremiah 17:8 that is planted by streams of water and does not fear when the heat comes. Its leaves are always green and it doesn't become anxious in a year of drought. We, too, can be certain, rather than anxious in times of financial insecurity, loss of our health, or loss of a loved one. We can bloom to our potential, bear much fruit, and become a source of food, shade, and refreshment for others. A future of intimacy with God means a future of fulfillment as we look to the Only One who satisfies and we live in the only way that satisfies.

A future of friendship

We saw in chapter 6 that an intimate relationship with Christ means finding our Best Friend. We've seen in chapters 2 through 5 that this Friend loves us and accepts us for who we are, that He will never leave us, that He sees us as beautiful in His eyes, and that we can approach Him openly and honestly about anything. We have a Constant Companion, a Forever Friend. And that is a reason to celebrate our future, because we can live it alongside One who sticks closer than a brother, closer than a lover, closer than a best friend.

A future of family

We learned in chapter 9 how God gives us a right to be His child, gives us a new family, and gives us a new lineage. We have a future of being able to call Him "Daddy," of having Him for a Husband, a Brother, a Father. So what do we lack? Intimacy with God means a sense of belonging and a future of family.

A future of shelter

God tells us in His Word that He is our refuge and strength, a very present help in trouble (Psalm 46:1). He is our Protector. Our Rock. Our Shield. And our Shelter (Psalm 18:30-31). He is the One whose arms we can run into when we are afraid, when we need assurance, when we seek protection from the things of this world that bombard us daily. He is our Strong Defender (Psalm 68:5 NIV), our Heavenly Husband who seeks to protect His precious bride. We looked in chapters 7 and 8 at the things that God loves and the things He hates, and one of the things He loves is taking care of us, His bride. One of the things He hates is anyone or anything that seeks to destroy us. In an intimate relationship with the Lord, we have a future of shelter amid the storms of life.

A future of dreams coming true

Not only can we experience the fulfillment of dreams here on earth that are realized by the grace of God (chapter 11), but we can only begin to fathom the wonders of our future with the Lord beyond this earth: no pain, tears, or sorrow; living in the light of His presence and the warmth of His love; walking on streets of gold; being His bride, well satisfied. It's a future we can only dream of. Our future in heaven will be one of eternal praise and pleasure in His presence.

WHERE ARE YOU GOING?

In the movie *Star Trek: Generations*, there was a planet, or a dimension, called "The Nexus" to which a scientist was obsessing to reach. One of the Star Trek *Enterprise* crew members who had been in "The Nexus" before being pulled away from it against her will described the experience: "It was like being inside joy—as if joy was something tangible and you could wrap yourself up in it like a blanket, and never in my entire life have I ever been so content."

That's the way I picture eternity with our Heavenly Husband. Being inside His arms must be something like being *inside joy*, wrapped up in Him snugly like a blanket and experiencing contentment like we've never known it. Psalm 16:11 tells us that in the Lord's presence there is fullness of joy and in His right hand there are pleasures forever. Imagine being in the arms of the Creator and

Perfector of Love, being so completely fulfilled that there is nowhere else you would ever want to be.

That is where you and I are when we remain in an intimate relationship with Jesus. There is no other place than in His arms where we can find contentment, fulfillment, and joy. Imagine being *inside True Love* as if it were a blanket you could wrap yourself up in. You will be—for eternity. And we have the rest of our days on this earth to get used to what we will experience in heaven with Him.

Are you looking for joy and a future in the arms of the Lord?

Lynn looked for joy in her career, her accomplishments, and her successes. She looked for it in her family and her dating relationships. But as time went by, she lost all of that. Even today she cannot find her ultimate fulfillment in Randy, as much as I'm sure he will try to be there for her. Her future and hope, as with all of us, comes from the Only One who can satisfy. The One who has her days numbered in His book, the One who wrote her future and has it in His hands, ready to give to her. He has our future in His hands as well, ready to unfold it for us as we live in intimacy with Him. But sometimes, like those women in the Old Testament, it's another future and another hope we seek.

GOD'S PLANS, NOT MY OWN

I remember the day when I believed my future was over. I believed it was mistakenly given to someone else and I no longer had hope. I missed it, lost out. And there was nothing left for me.

I'd just discovered that Mike—the man I'd wanted all my life—had married someone else. I met Mike as a child at a Christian conference center on the Oregon coast. I believed, at the age of nine, that we were meant for each other. And I dreamed for years of someday being his bride. We met each other again as teenagers and I was impressed at the fine young man he had become. He had a real commitment to Christ that I hadn't seen in a man his age and he gave me a glimpse of what it would be like to be loved by a man who truly loved God and therefore would know how to truly love a woman.

As Mike and I kept in touch during our high-school and college years, I believed the Holy Spirit was drawing the two of us together for a glorious future we couldn't begin to fathom. We talked vaguely of future plans together and of what incredible things God might have in store for us. But through a series of events that were out of my control (and which I now believe were God-ordained), Mike asked another woman to be his partner for life. The extent to which he moved across the country in his military training and the speed at which things fell together for him and an old girlfriend back home left me unable to compete or catch up.

In a foolish last-ditch attempt, I penned a letter to him, pleading with him to change his mind and realize that it was God's will for us to be together. But Mike's heart and head led him in another direction.

The day I discovered he had gotten married, I was devastated. *Had God forgotten about me? Why didn't God choose to intervene with Mike's plans and bring his heart back around to me? What future could I possibly have now, apart from the one man I had wanted all my life?*

But God *had* a future and a hope for me. However, it wasn't the future I had tried to work out. It wasn't the hope I had come to pursue. God's future for me led me not to the East coast to be a Marine's wife, but to the California desert to be a minister's wife. God's plans were not to *give me* the one I had lived for, but to *become* the One I would live for. By leading me to Hugh, a man who didn't talk openly about his feelings as Mike had, I learned to seek closeness and intimacy with God. By putting me alongside a pastor—whose life largely involved ministering to others, and not necessarily me—I learned to be a woman who was not so consumed with my own needs. And by living with a man who encouraged me to love God more than anyone else, I learned to rely on the Lord, not my husband, to meet my deepest emotional needs. Through our marriage, Hugh and I have learned that the key to our intimacy with each other is how well each of us is intimately connected with God. God has always been and will always be determined to be the middle man through which Hugh and I will love each other and enjoy life together. And I realize now that the Lord, my True Love, had always sought me with an even stronger passion than that which I had experienced for Mike.

Sometimes I still wonder what my future with Mike would've held. Would we have been more harmonious? Would we have been more compatible? But I rest in the wisdom and sovereignty of my Heavenly Husband in directing me to the man he did—a marriage and a future in which I could grow, develop, and experience the fullness of God. The glorious future God had for me was not one with Mike, whom my heart longed for, but it was one with Himself, whom my heart now longs for...and the One with whom I can say I have finally found my heart's hunger satisfied. In His own perfect way, God truly *was* leading me to a glorious future that I couldn't begin to fathom.

FACING YOUR FUTURE

Perhaps you're living a future right now that you didn't intend. Maybe your hopes for a happily ever after with someone didn't pan out. There will be times when all of us, like Lynn, find it difficult to walk the path in front of us. Our steps sometimes are so uncertain we're unsure if we'll be able to make it. But focusing our eyes on the One who awaits us can help us walk confidently and smile at our future. Focusing on Him will remind us that our future is not about what we have or don't have, or about what might happen or what might not happen. Our future is all about Who we know and how well we know Him.

When we focus on the One we know intimately, the things that seem to threaten our happily ever after fade into the shadow of His presence. After all, how can we fear our financial situation when we know intimately the One who owns the cattle on a thousand hills?[8] Why should we worry about what we have or don't have when God promises us in Philippians 4:19 that He will supply all our needs according to His riches in Christ Jesus? *No longer will you feel the rain of financial worries, for I will be your Shelter.*

We no longer need to be frightened or discouraged by health concerns when we know intimately the Great Physician. We can rest in the assurance that nothing will touch our bodies or interrupt the beating of our heart or enter the blood that runs through our veins without first passing through the sovereign, loving hands of our Lord. God promises that all things—even things concerning our health—work together for good to those who love Him so that we can be conformed to the image of His Son (Romans 8:28-29). *No longer will you feel the cold fear of losing your health, for I will be your warmth.*

And why should we fear a future of loneliness when we know intimately a Heavenly Husband who promises He will never leave us or desert us? Why should we fear raising children alone when our True Love has promised to be a husband to the husbandless and a father to the fatherless?[9] *No longer will you face the pain of loneliness, for I will be your comfort.*

FOCUSING ON A FUTURE TOGETHER

My friend, your future is all about Who you know and the benefits of knowing Him. Your future truly is a happily ever after when it is lived in intimacy with the One who loves you more than any other.

Our intimacy with God doesn't mean there will be no storms, but that we will be sheltered in those storms. Our future with Him doesn't mean we will never get cold, but that His warmth will be available when the cold front blows in. Our future with Him doesn't guarantee He will bring someone to our side so we'll never be alone, but that we will sense His presence and comfort in the loneliness.

God promises us in His Word that seeking a future of intimacy with Him is far better than hoping for a happily ever after in anything the world can offer—be it princes, palaces, or pleasures.

In Psalm 118:9 He tenderly tells us, "It is better to take refuge in the LORD than to trust in princes."

Are you taking refuge in the One who has committed Himself to you for life? Is the Lord the One you are trusting in for your future? Are you satisfied with Him being the Prince who can whisk you away to a more fulfilled life? I hope so. Because only in Him can you experience a happily ever after.

Experience it now—and forever.

Celebrating Your Future

❦

Your happily ever after begins today. Embrace the love He offers you, celebrate the life that lies ahead of you, and live for the Lover who awaits you. As you work through these steps, experience—and celebrate—the future that awaits you in the arms of True Love.

1. Are there still some things you would like to see happen in your future for you to be fulfilled? Name these things before the Lord, asking Him to become the focus of your future and all you seek. God does promise you a life of fulfillment when He is the object of your search (Psalm 37:4).

2. What are your life goals for your future with your Heavenly Husband? Where do you want to be in your relationship with Him at the end of your days here on earth? How do you want to spend the time you have left? What will you do to go the distance with Him in a way that positively affects your future?

3. What are three things you can do this week to invest in your eternal future with the Lord?

4. What are some things you can do to invest in your future right now with the Lord?

A Parting Encouragement:

Giving Him Your All

You have made it, my friend. You have found what most women search for all their lives. You have surpassed the realm of trusting God with your eternal life and entered the arena of trusting Him with your everyday life and your emotional life. In doing so, you have become a woman who never needs to look anywhere else for fulfillment, significance, or love. Stay within His embrace and experience a happily ever after—a life lived in intimacy with the Lover of your soul.

As you feast on His banquet of love, rejoice in the fact that you will never go hungry again. Experience the joy of being filled, satisfied, and longing no more. How can you be otherwise? You have found True Love!

Notes

Chapter 1—Finding the One Who Will Satisfy

1. Genesis 1:18-22.
2. In 2 Corinthians 5:17, we are told we are new creatures in Christ and our past is forgotten.
3. In the latter part of Hebrews 13:5, we are told that Jesus will never leave us nor desert us.
4. In Psalm 139:23, David invites God, his Creator, to search his heart and thoughts.
5. Hebrews 4:14-16 says Jesus is one who can sympathize with us and therefore, we need not be intimidated about approaching Him. Instead, we are told to "draw near [Him] with confidence."
6. Jesus said in John 15:13, "Greater love has no one than this, that one lay down his life for his friends." Jesus later did just that, laying down His life for us upon a cross of crucifixion.
7. David, who knew God intimately, said in Psalm 65:2, "O Thou who dost hear prayer, to Thee all men come."
8. Psalm 16:5-6 says, "The LORD is the portion of my inheritance and my cup; Thou dost support my lot. The lines have fallen to me in pleasant places; indeed, my heritage is beautiful to me.
9. According to Ephesians 2:10, each of us is created for good deeds that God has already planned for us to accomplish.
10. Jeremiah 29:11 says, "I know the plans that I have for you,' declares the LORD, 'plans for welfare and not for calamity to give you a future and a hope.' "

Chapter 2—Knowing He Accepts Me

1. John 4:5-26.
2. Romans 5:18-19.
3. See also Hebrews 8:12 and Hebrews 10:17.
4. Psalm 139:13, 15-16.
5. Romans 6:1-2 says, "Are we to continue in sin that grace might increase? May it never be!" See also verses 14-15.
6. John 8:1-11.
7. Psalm 139:23-24.

Chapter 3—Realizing He'll Never Leave

1. Psalm 77:19.
2. Genesis 16:1-15.
3. John 10:10-16,27.
4. Matthew 18:12-14.
5. Jeremiah 29:11.
6. Cynthia Heald, *Becoming a Woman of Purpose* (Colorado Springs, CO: NavPress, 1994), p. 36.

Chapter 4—Understanding How He Sees Me

1. 2 Corinthians 5:17.
2. Hebrews 11:6.
3. 1 Peter 3:3-5.

Chapter 5—Approaching Him with Confidence

1. Deuteronomy 4:31.
2. Referring to Jesus Christ as our "high priest," Hebrews 4:15 says, "We do not have a high priest who cannot sympathize with our weaknesses, but One who has been tempted in all things as we are, yet without sin."
3. 1 Samuel 1:1-20.
4. John 11:21.
5. John 11:32-33.
6. John 21:1-19.

7. O. Hallesby, *Prayer* (London: InterVarsity, 1959), pp. 39-40.

8. James 1:6-8.

9. Hallesby, ibid.

Chapter 6—*Making Him My Best Friend*

1. 2 Timothy 2:13 says, "If we are faithless, He remains faithful; for He cannot deny Himself."

2. In John 14:23 Jesus said, "If anyone loves Me, he will keep My word."

3. Isaiah 55:8-9 says that God's thoughts and His methods of doing things are very different than ours.

4. Psalm 139:7-10.

5. Luke 18:1-5.

6. Genesis 5:22-24; Hebrews 11:5.

7. "In the Garden" by C. Austin Miles (Hall-Mack Co., 1912; Renewed 1940, The Rodeheaver Co.).

Chapter 7—*Clinging to What He Desires*

1. Acts 13:22.

2. Job 1:8.

3. Luke 1:28.

4. Luke 8:1-3.

5. Matthew 27:55-56.

6. Matthew 27:57-61.

7. Mark 16:9; John 20:10-18.

8. Luke 10:38-42.

9. John 11:32-35.

10. John 12:1-3.

11. Matthew 26:13; Mark 14:9.

12. Hebrews 11:1.

13. *The American Heritage Dictionary* (Boston, MA: Houghton Mifflin Co., 1985), p. 319.

14. Ibid., p. 745.

15. 2 Corinthians 9:7.

Chapter 8—Avoiding What He Dislikes

1. Psalm 51:10-11.
2. 2 Samuel 11–12:14.
3. Eugene H. Peterson, *The Message: The New Testament, Psalms and Proverbs in Contemporary Language* (Colorado Springs, CO: NavPress, 1993), p. 757.
4. Isaiah 14:12-15.
5. Genesis 3:1-19.
6. Numbers 20:9-12.
7. Acts 5:1-10.
8. 1 Corinthians 13:7.

Chapter 9—Listening to His Loving Voice

1. Luke 19:1-5.
2. See Song of Songs 6:3.

Chapter 10—Discovering a New Lineage

1. Isaiah 66:13.
2. Naomi describes Boaz as "one of our closest relatives" in Ruth 2:20, but the literal meaning of the original Hebrew text is "redeemer." Thus we get the term "kinsman redeemer."
3. Ruth 4:21-22 (Matthew 1:5-16 traces Jesus' geneology back to Boaz and Ruth).
4. Romans 8:15.
5. Galatians 4:1-7 and Ephesians 1:5 explain this adoption.
6. 1 Peter 5:4; Revelation 4:9-11.
7. Mark 14:36.
8. Romans 8:31.

Chapter 11—Living with a New Purpose

1. Jeremiah 17:5-6.
2 Jeremiah 17:7-8.

3. Matthew 5:16.

4. 2 Timothy 2:15 (KJV).

Chapter 12—Experiencing a Future Together

1. Psalm 18:30 (NIV).

2. Genesis 3.

3. Genesis 16:1-6 (in Genesis 17:15, God changed Sarai's name to Sarah).

4. Genesis 24.

5. Genesis 25:21-23.

6. Genesis 27:1-17.

7. Genesis 29:30–30:24.

8. Psalm 50:10.

9. Psalm 68:5.

An Invitation to Write

Cindi McMenamin has a passion for encouraging, inspiring, and motivating women to become intimate with God. If you would like to have Cindi speak to your group or if you would like to share with Cindi how God has used *Heart Hunger* in your life, write:

Cindi McMenamin
c/o Harvest House Publishers
1075 Arrowsmith
Eugene, Oregon 97402
or e-mail: hcmcmen@pe.net

Other Harvest House Reading

• *A Woman After God's Own Heart*
by Elizabeth George
If you want to achieve a growing relationship with God, develop an active partnership with your husband, and make your home into a spiritual oasis, you'll want to read this book! Discover how to become the woman of excellence God designed you to be.

• *Women Who Loved God*
by Elizabeth George
Women Who Loved God, a 365-day devotional, is a perfect way for you to begin or end your day. An excellent companion for individual Bible studies, mentoring relationships, or your prayer groups and Bible studies.

• *A Woman God Can Use*
by Pam Farrel
This book attunes us to hear the applause of heaven as never before. By exchanging the fleeting standards of the world for the steadfast truths of the Bible, you will find yourself being free to become a woman God can use.

• *Quiet Moments for Mothers*
by Joyce & H. Norman Wright
This charming collection of inspirational quotes from Elisabeth Elliot, Rudyard Kipling, Hannah Whitall Smith, and others honors motherhood.